N.

With good wishes

T.

COLLECTING BIRD STAMPS

Books by the same author
BRITISH NAMES OF BIRDS
BIRD ILLUSTRATORS

SOME WELL-DESIGNED BIRD PORTRAITS

Turks & Caicos 1973, Flamingo; Montserrat 1970, Purple-throated Carib; B.I.O.T. 1975, Red-headed Forest Fody; Surinam 1977, Hawk-headed Parrot; Saint Lucia 1976, Osprey; Guyana 1968, Cock of the Rock; India 1975, Western Tragopan; Ghana 1961, Giant Plantain-eater; Seychelles 1976, Paradise Flycatcher; U.S.A. 1972, Cardinal; Bahamas 1974, Roseate Spoonbills.

Collecting
BIRD STAMPS

CHRISTINE E. JACKSON

H. F. & G. WITHERBY LTD.

First published in 1977 by
H. F. & G. WITHERBY LTD.
5 Plantain Place, Crosby Row,
London SE1 1YN
© Christine E. Jackson, 1977
ISBN 0 85493 126 0
Filmset in 11pt. Times
and printed by Ebenezer Baylis and Son Ltd.,
The Trinity Press, Worcester, and London

This book is dedicated to
Timothy John Sture and
Timothy Martin Jones

Contents

Grenada, Belted Kingfisher, issued 1976

Full-page Illustrations

Acknowledgements

Mr Anthony Grainger (of 42 Lee Lane East, Horsforth, Leeds, Yorkshire), a specialist bird stamp dealer, has been most kind and helpful in reading through the manuscript of this book and made many useful suggestions and corrections. I am most grateful to him and welcome this opportunity to thank him for his assistance and also for generously sharing his detailed knowledge of bird stamps. Any remaining errors or controversial opinions are my responsibility.

James Negus of Stanley Gibbons Publications Ltd., kindly gave assistance with details of their catalogues.

I am indebted to Thomas Nelson & Son, the publishers of *A New Dictionary of Birds* by A. L. Thomson, for permission to reproduce the map on page 31.

My publisher, Mr Antony Witherby is unfailingly patient and painstaking and I am happy to acknowledge my appreciation of his encouragement and the skill with which he transforms an untidy manuscript into a well-produced book.

I also wish to thank my husband, Andrew B. Jackson, for his interest in my bird stamp collection, the progress of the manuscript and his assistance in selecting the designs to be illustrated.

Part of a definitive set of 16 stamps, all depicting birds,
issued by St. Lucia in 1976.

1

A Chapter for Beginners

This chapter is intended for the person contemplating collecting bird stamps, and for those who have already started but are bewildered by the vast number of stamps available and wonder how they should be selected and purchased.

What is available?
The large number of stamps depicting birds will surprise many people. There are over 3,400 stamps depicting identifiable species as their main subject, and at least another 1,000 with domestic or stylised birds and birds incidental to the main non-ornithological motif on the stamp.

The first bird stamp was issued from Basle, Switzerland, and depicted a "dove". This 1845 stamp was also the first stamp in the world to be printed in more than one colour. Now we have reached the stage where over one hundred new bird stamps are issued every year. Some of them are issued singly, some in short sets of four to eight, others in longer sets. A few bird sets form the country's definitive set of stamps (i.e. stamps specifically issued for ordinary postal needs and placed on sale for an unlimited period). More often, birds form the subject of commemorative stamps, or are issued to provide income for a charity. Both commemorative and charity stamps are sold for a limited period and concurrently with the definitive stamps.

The stamps themselves vary considerably in quality of design and reproduction. There are some grossly inaccurate pictures of birds, and, at the opposite extreme, some exquisitely beautiful miniature portraits with every colour and line faithfully reproduced. Some birds are depicted in monochrome, whilst others are printed in one, two or many colours. Occasionally the colours are quite inappropriate, but more often they are close to the genuine colouring of the feathers.

Availability of stamps also varies—the Commonwealth countries' bird stamps are relatively easy to obtain, and so are those of the countries with whom we trade. The early issues of some foreign colonies are not so easily procured from British dealers, but since the business of buying, selling and collecting stamps has been established for so long in this country, we are better equipped to deal with "difficult" countries than most. Some countries over-produce pictorial stamps. They issue far more than they require for their postal needs, and flood the market with them. We'll deal with this subject later.

How the birds are chosen by designers and artists frequently remains unknown. If a set is labelled "Zoo Birds" or "Rare Birds" or "Nature Conservation" we have a clue, but there are many more sets which include birds and the reasons for the choice of those species illustrated are obscure. Why, for instance, are Count Raggi's Bird of Paradise and the very similar Great Bird of Paradise (it is not always clear which was intended by the artist) the most frequently pictured species on bird stamps. They appear on over 80 stamps. If we make a list of the next top ten birds, they are 54 Kagus, 48 Black Swans, 44 Andean Condors or Vultures, 36 Flamingoes, 34 Peregrines, 33 Southern Lapwings, 31 Golden Eagles, 29 Crowned Cranes and 29 White Storks, 27 Quetzals and 27 Hoopoes, 22 Golden Orioles and 22 Ostriches, 20 Mallards Secretary Birds and Pheasant. These I counted to the end of 1974 and included only those stamps where the bird forms the main feature of the design and is clearly identifiable. Some of these birds appear in many parts of the world and so several countries have depicted them, but many are not immediately recognisable as candidates for such popular appeal. The Kagu, Quetzal, Andean Condors and Greater Bird of Paradise are virtually national emblem birds, hence their repetitive use by New Caledonia, Guatemala, Chile, Papua & New Guinea respectively. But

Part of the definitive set, Botswana 1967: 1c Golden Oriole; 2c African Hoopoe; 3c Ground Scraper Thrush; 4c Blue Waxbill; 5c Secretary Bird.

New Zealand Health Stamp 1964, Red-billed Gull; Swiss Children's Charity Stamp 1970, Hoopoe; Ghana Commemorative Stamp 1957, Palmnut Vulture.

the others are not so easily explained. On the other hand, there are equally picturesque and eye-catching species which have only one stamp, and hundreds of attractive species which have never appeared on stamps.

Knowing what species have appeared, and in what quantity, may well help you in deciding which group of birds you would like to collect. To find out which species have appeared in order to make such a choice, you can consult W. F. Stanley's booklet, *Birds of the World on Stamps*, which provides a complete list up to the end of 1972.

*Guatemala 1881, Quetzal
A bird of the tropical forests*

What do they cost?

Prices vary from 1 penny to over £100 for one stamp. Before selecting a special area or group of birds whose stamps will form your collection, it would be as well to look at the cost of the stamps you will need to purchase. Stanley Gibbons publish a world catalogue of stamps each year with the latest price against each stamp listed. Generally speaking, the Air stamps cost the most, and the Air stamps frequently depict the rarest birds of the country or the most majestic "expensive-looking" birds such as eagles. You will not find the common little House Sparrow on the stamps of the highest value—there is a curious kind of ornithological snobbery at work here! Other very expensive bird stamps are those issued before 1875 which form part of classical bird sets e.g. the Western Australian stamps depicting Swans, issued 1854 onwards, which mint can fetch £200+ each, and even the more numerous later issues can cost £20. Working through the Gibbons' catalogue is the only way to sort these out. "Used" examples, of some, are not so costly.

Having dealt with those which are expensive, let me hasten to reassure a would-be collector that there are far more inexpensive stamps than there are expensive ones. Frequently the modern and less expensive stamps are more attractively produced than the earlier stamps depicting birds which are also

Three countries which have used Eagles for their Air stamps: Senegal 1960 African Fish Eagle; Liberia 1938 Steller's(?) Eagle; U.S.A. 1963 Bald Eagle.

the most expensive ones to buy. One of the great blessings of this hobby is that you can spend as little or as much as you like, and whatever you spend, you will have an attractive picture gallery of birds which is both colourful, varied in shape and size of stamp, and a great pleasure to own and look at. For a few pence you can start a collection, and then add to it gradually or quickly according to your inclination and the depth of your pocket. At the moment it would cost a person £20 to £30 to buy all the bird stamps issued in one year. It is unlikely, however, that you will want to just buy the issues of each year, dating from when you first take an interest in bird stamps. You will almost certainly want to do some retrospective buying. The fact that there are so many already available, and that the cost of keeping up with new issues is likely to increase (since inflation is a world-wide disease), make it more than likely that you will want to be selective in your collecting of bird stamps, rather than collect comprehensively. In the following chapters I have outlined some selective bird stamp collections which might appeal to you, and would cost a great deal less than a comprehensive collection. I have also indicated how many stamps are involved, because it is useful to know what size of collection you would eventually have.

The prices listed by Gibbons in their catalogues are the prices you would pay for mounted mint stamps and very lightly franked used stamps. Not all stamps are in such condition, since used stamps may be found in all states from lightly franked to having the picture of the bird obliterated by the franking machine. The price of used stamps will there-fore vary from the Gibbons' price quite considerably, according to the assessment of your dealer. You may have to pay the Gibbons' price for mint stamps, but many dealers obtain their mint stamps in bulk and sell at less than cata-logue prices, so it pays to shop around. The cost of non-British Commonwealth stamps when purchased from a dealer may differ rather more from the Gibbons' price than the cost of Commonwealth stamps. The most important factor is the condition of the stamp which should be clean and without a crease or tear if used, and perfect down to the last corner of the perforations, if mint, and should be well-centred.

This brings us to the question whether to collect stamps in mint condition, or stamps which have been through the postal system and are "used".

Mint or used?

There are advantages and disadvantages to both types of collecting, but for neither of them is there a certainty that one will increase in value more than the other. A glance at the price of old stamps in Gibbons' catalogues will confirm this. Some used copies are not in plentiful supply and so their value is now higher than a mint copy of the same stamp. Conversely, a large number of used copies on the market will deflate their price and make that of the mint stamp higher.

This being so, perhaps we should be guided by quite a different consideration than the monetary value of the stamps. If we buy a bird stamp for the sake of the picture of the bird printed on that stamp, then it is better that it should be clean, new and undefaced. The disadvantage to this, is that sometimes it is nearly impossible to obtain a mint copy, or else the used copy is very much cheaper. Then a difficult decision has to be made, to mix mint and used, or to do without certain items.

One of the gravest disadvantages to collecting used stamps is the vexed problem of "C.T.O." sets. A number of countries print vast quantities of pictorials and then, without actually sending them through the post, they press a cancellation stamp over one corner of each pictorial and sell it as a "used" stamp. Stamps treated in this way are known in the trade as "Cancelled to Order". Gum on the back of cancelled to order stamps points to their not having been through the post and are a give-away clue to the fact that they are not genuine used stamps. (However, lack of gum on the back of a stamp does not prove that it has been through the postal service since some stamps are issued gumless!)

Cancelled to order stamps should be treated with caution and the advice of your dealer sought. Many countries issue cancelled stamps, but there is a subtle difference between those issued by British Commonwealth countries and those issued by East European countries, which should be noted. The British Commonwealth cancelled to order stamps are normally sold at face value, whilst those from the East European countries are usually available at a price less than face value.

Some collectors prefer to have their stamps still attached to the envelopes which carried them through the mail. This way there is no question as to their authenticity as "used" stamps, and a collection of envelopes adds another dimension to stamp collecting.

A mint and used copy of the Bechuanaland 2½c 1961 Scarlet-chested Sunbird.
Cancelled to order ½b Yemen 1970 Peacock.

Countries indulge in all kinds of other issuing devices, though these are legitimate. Sometimes the same design is repeated, with a change of currency, e.g. many of these occurred when Commonwealth countries changed from pence (d) to decimal currency. Sometimes the unsold original currency stamps are overprinted with the new currency such as the ¼d crossed through and alongside it ¼c printed, in the Cayman Islands stamps depicting the Cayman Island Thrush.

Change of currency from old ¼d to new ¼c Cayman Island Thrush, 1969–70.

When a country is celebrating a national event, such as Independence Day, those words may be overprinted on the stamps sold for a short period on and after the date of independence day. These devices add to the number of stamps available for purchase and provide interesting information about a country's history and activities. They also raise the question as to whether a bird stamp collector wants an example of each variant in his collection, or if he is going to purchase just one copy of that stamp—perhaps the original issue which will be the least printed upon and therefore the least defaced. Frequently the wording is printed over the picture of the bird. Again, it is a matter of personal choice, and that choice might well be decided on either economic or aesthetic grounds.

Overprinted stamps with picture of Great Kiskadee defaced. British Honduras 4c of 1964 and 1965.

There are also some bird stamp forgeries, but mercifully these are not numerous. Some books about forgeries have been published and these can be sorted through to pick out bird stamp forgeries. The most frequently quoted example of a forgery is the George VI & Peacock of Burma 1938 (1 and 2 rupee values), but these stamps could be avoided by excluding them altogether from your collection for the reason that the peacock is not the main motif on the stamp.

A few "phantom" stamp sets have appeared on the market. These are issued by imaginary countries or small states with no right to issue stamps. "Thomond" sets exist, though no country of that name may be found. The stamps depict a finch, a martin, hummingbirds and a seabird among others. There is also a set from Maluku Selatan of the South Moluccas (seceded from Indonesia in 1950) whose status is uncertain and stamps of doubtful validity. In addition, there are spurious sets from Ajman and Sharjah which appeared on the market after those countries ceased to issue their own stamps, 1st August 1972, upon becoming part of the United Arab Emirates.

Phantom stamps of Maluku Selatan—part of set.

What is a bird stamp?

It is time we clarified this point, and yet it is so much a matter of individual choice that I have left it until now to discuss. A purist would require his bird stamp to have as the main, and only motif, a clear correctly coloured and accurate representation of a recognisable species of wild bird. This cuts out a large number of stamps, but leaves a nucleus of excellent quality stamps well worth seeking and owning.

A broader definition could be adopted, so that stamps bearing a large enough portrait of a bird for its species to be recognised without doubt, would be included, even if the bird were not the only or main feature of the stamp design. A large number of stamps portray a bird in one half of their surface area, and if these are recognisable portraits, there is no point in deliberately ignoring them except where an otherwise too large collection would be assembled.

An excellent bird stamp, Lesotho 1970 Blue Korhaan, designed by Richard Granger Barrett.

An acceptable bird stamp, B.I.O.T. 1971 (Opening of R.S. Research Station Aldabra) and Aldabran White-throated Rail.

Unsatisfactory as a bird stamp, British Guiana 1954 Victoria Regia Lilies and Wattled Jacana (or Lily trotters).

If the challenge of collecting and attempting to identify the many ''unidentified flying objects'' on stamps appeals to you, there is no reason why you should not include them and classify as you think fit, or keep them separate and have occasional sessions with them when you feel in a Sherlock Holmes mood.

In Chapter 6 this question of what is a bird stamp is dealt with more fully, but it is important from the very commencement of your selecting and buying, to form a clear idea of what your standard is to be, and to write it down, and adhere to it strictly. Otherwise a remarkable hotch-potch of stamps of varying quality will accrue and might eventually even annoy its owner, especially if he is a keen bird-man.

The Quality of Bird Stamps

Some stamps are referred to by philatelists as "classics", some are regarded as "rubbish", and there are many in between which are not called anything in particular. The classics are, generally speaking, those early issues published before 1875 and are mostly very expensive to buy because they are eagerly sought after and in short supply. The term is also sometimes applied to later issues than 1875 which have now some rarity value. Few bird stamps are classics. The in-between material is well worth collecting, and is reasonably priced with some odd exceptions. Rubbish, I am afraid, abounds among bird stamps. You will not find this term defined in a dictionary of philatelist's terms, but seasoned stamp-collectors know it means some "cancelled to order" items, and stamps issued in numbers far in excess of a country's postal needs. Stanley Gibbons has wearied of listing "rubbish" and you will find their attitude to it plainly revealed in the Appendix at the back of the *Stamps of the World* catalogue in which those countries' sets which are in excess of their postal requirements are merely listed by date of issue and number of values. We might also include many of the pictorials issued by some Eastern communist countries, and by some South American countries and a lot of Arab states.

A newcomer, seeing that a certain country has issued a lot of bird stamps, would be forgiven for eagerly collecting those pictorials as easy material for a beginner, but this is just the material of which he should beware. It is cheap now, and it will always be comparatively cheap because know-ledgeable collectors do not want it. There is another consideration. Cuba has issued more bird stamps than any other country, but it has done so just to sell the stamps abroad to collectors for revenue and not for its own postal use. Do we wish to encourage this type of postal authority?

There is no need to purchase complete sets in which the bird stamps only form a part, the rest of the set being made up of animals, flowers, shells, etc. It is possible to buy only the bird stamps from mixed sets and a specialist dealer is the best source for these.

Some sets are not only beautiful, but they will almost certainly increase in value—if only to keep pace with inflation. A country's definitive set depicting birds is well worth buying, and never miss a new set which, although it might initially cost £6–£8, is of excellent design and craftsmanship. The chapter on artists and designers will give you a good idea of some issues which will be regarded as twentieth century classics some day.

Where to buy stamps

A specialist dealer is usually the best source in the long run, but they are few and far between. There is a bird stamp dealer who advertises in the R.S.P.B. magazine *Birds*, and you may find others in stamp magazines.

Some firms dealing in a wide range of subjects offer thematic collections on approval and will send a package at intervals to suit your requirements. There is also a possibility of buying bulk packages—of say 100 or 500 bird stamps. These sound attractive and can be useful for a beginner to familiarise him with the variety of stamps available. Collecting over a broad spectrum, this might be a good way to start, but many collectors would prefer to make their own selection rather than select from someone else's selection as well as being left with a pile of unwanted material. The packets rarely contain complete sets and the remaining half or quarter of a set will have to be sought elsewhere. The stamps in bulk packets are usually used, and mainly from the cheaper end of the trade. If you collect selectively, there will be a very small percentage of items you will want from a bulk packet.

Auction lots can sometimes be obtained—and at reasonable prices. They would give a beginner, with a broad subject approach, a good nucleus collection to start building on. The same objections apply, however, as to bulk packet buying.

Local stamp dealers are sometimes sympathetic towards a thematic collector and are helpful in putting "birds" on one

Examples of well-designed bird stamps.

side. Through a local dealer, new issues can be ordered in advance, and specific items ordered from a catalogue. Dealing with a local man also has the advantage of your being able to see the standard of his business and quality of his stamps before committing yourself. The first few visits will be exciting because you can sort through retrospective issues which he has in his stock. When you have exhausted that stock, you will most probably want to go and explore other dealers' stamps. However, buying from one or two reliable dealers who are sympathetic towards your rather special requirements is the most satisfactory way of buying locally.

Local newsagents' sealed packets of stamps are to be avoided, however tempting they may appear. The packets usually contain poor material such as that listed in the Appendix to Gibbons' *Stamps of the World* catalogue and the sets are frequently incomplete—the top or highest values not being included. They also contain cancelled to order material.

Joining a stamp club if there is one in your area (ask at the library and search the local newspaper) is one of the best ways to get the most out of collecting stamps. The chance to talk to other enthusiasts is always a pleasure, and you can exchange information and sometimes also swap stamps. The splitting up of zoo sets with someone else taking the animals and reptiles off your hands, is yet another advantage to club membership. Some clubs publish bulletins which might contain articles of use to you.

How to buy stamps

It is not easy to buy stamps to a given programme, they are not always immediately available, or a new issue which you need empties the kitty unexpectedly. However, it is wise to have a flexible plan on the lines of what you need most, what it would be nice to have some time, and what can be left indefinitely. Otherwise, you'll get hopelessly side-tracked by collector's fever or some such unpleasantly overpowering impulse which you will later regret.

One golden rule, which I wish I had obeyed myself, is "If in doubt, leave it out". It can nearly always be got at a later date, and there is usually something more important near at hand.

Is a Bird Stamp Collection a good Investment?

Some individual stamps in a bird stamp collection could turn out to be a good investment for reasons of scarcity. However, your collection will include many stamps of low value which, over a period of years, are unlikely to do more than keep pace with inflation. So it would be best to collect for the fun of the hobby, expecting no return other than the interest you acquire in the hobby itself. If the stamp collection does prove eventually to have been a good investment, then regard that as a bonus. But remember that a collection of mint stamps in the finest condition which has been kept unmounted will hold its value better as the years go by, and if you sell your stamps as a collection you may get your money back and make a modest profit. An unmounted collection of mint stamps will always have a higher re-sale value than a collection of mounted stamps. However, if you want to enjoy stamp collecting, collect birds on stamps, put them in your album, arrange and re-arrange them if you want to, and look at them often, and to ensure that you enjoy them to the maximum—forget what you paid for them.

Equipment required

Starting with a small amount of equipment gives one the opportunity to abandon a project if it proves to be unsatisfactory in any way. So start with some album leaves, and hinges which peel off easily (since some remounting inevitably occurs). It is as well to allocate space very generously from the commencement of the mounting of your stamps. This seems wasteful of paper, but will save a lot of handling, remounting and re-labelling of album leaves at a later stage.

As the collection grows, the spring back, or other type of album, can be purchased to keep the leaves together. The minimum size of the album should be $11\frac{1}{2}'' \times 10''$. Some small etceteras are, a book to keep unclassified and as yet unmounted stamps clean and flat, a pair of tweezers to save handling the stamps with the fingers, and a magnifying glass.

A loose-leaf file is useful to compile your own list of stamps which fall within the subject of your choice. A card index or another loose-leaf file will be added later for writing notes about the stamps in your collection, but that can wait awhile.

If you collect mint stamps and do not wish to mount them, you can purchase black or clear background mounts with transparent strips which allow the stamps to be slotted into position behind a strip of plastic material which holds them in place and at the same time shields them from dust and prevents hinge damage.

Books and Periodicals
It is better not to purchase any book until you are familiar with it, and have found it answers your questions and contains the information you need. Your public library is sure to stock many books on both stamps and stamp collecting; about countries, their history and geography; atlases and bird books. A library will normally subscribe to, and display, a stamp periodical or journal. In the reference section you will find the latest Gibbons' *Stamps of the World* catalogue and you may also be allowed to borrow a copy of that and other Gibbons' catalogues. If the current edition is not available for loan, ask if earlier editions are in the storeroom behind the scenes, and start working on those, then get up to date with the last year or two from the reference copy by working on it for a short time in the Reference Library.

Having read the issues of Gibbons' *Stamp Monthly* and other stamp magazines as they are published, you can choose which magazine seems most suited to your particular requirements and order it from your local newsagent.

I have not given prices for books recommended as these change so frequently, and some of them are out of print.

At this stage I particularly recommend you to borrow, and perhaps buy having seen it, Willard F. Stanley (and others) *Birds of the World on Stamps*, published in 1974 (Handbook no. 82 of American Topical Association, 3306 North 50th Street. Milwaukee, Wis. 53216. Obtainable from some stamp dealers in Britain.)

Studies in bird flight.

2

Comprehensive and selective collecting of bird stamps

Most people collect bird stamps, initially, in a haphazard manner. They might be given someone else's stamp collection and find the birds particularly attractive, extract them, and so start collecting bird stamps to add to that small nucleus collection picked at random. This is added to when relatives and friends pass on used stamps from their mail, and packets of stamps are purchased. Some will go on to add more stamps and perhaps just buy sets which appeal to them most, but with no systematic approach or organised thought on the matter.

Let us assume, for the moment, that a collector is content to mount his bird stamps as and when they come to hand—having no inclination to spend more time on them. It is unlikely that he will ever own all 3,000+ bird stamps, so there is no need to work out in detail the amount of space needed for mounting, but he will need to have a flexible system so that new stamps may be inserted without causing disruption and remounting.

The simplest method of organising such a collection is by country, and date of issue. The album leaf bears the name of the country as a heading, and is filed in the album in alphabetical order of the country's name. The leaves carry sets of stamps with a note of the date and event they commemorate, written neatly on the leaf near the set. In order to keep a record of what is already in the collection so that duplicates are not purchased, a marked-up copy of a catalogue, one of Gibbons' or W. F. Stanley's *Birds of the World on Stamps* (the section arranged by country) can be kept and taken on shopping expeditions. Alternatively, a personal index may be compiled in which each country's stamps which you wish to purchase are listed, in date order, on a single sheet, and the sheets filed alphabetically. Marking off the stamps you already own means you can keep a record of them without having to carry albums around. It also reveals at a glance what is required to be purchased. In addition, making your own list means that you can leave out peace doves, porcelain ducks, stylised birds and all the other non-wild species depicted on stamps, if that is your policy.

The advantages of this system of collecting are that it is simple, flexible, sets are kept together, and se-tenant stamps (i.e. 2 stamps issued joined together) need not be separated. However, this kind of collecting tells you very little about the country or the birds it has depicted on its stamps. The bird stamps are only a fraction of the postal output of a country, whose history cannot possibly be deduced from them. Even the birds chosen to be depicted are not necessarily those species which either breed or winter in that country, since many countries issue zoo sets, rare bird sets and even extinct bird sets.

An alternative arrangement is by the birds themselves. This requires a great deal more work and research, and some knowledge of birds and their families, etc. Again, Stanley's *Birds of the World on Stamps* provides the basis in the classified list of bird stamps arranged by bird orders, families, genera, and species. Mounting the stamps on album leaves, each one of which is devoted to a single species, takes a lot more time, patience—and album leaves. The leaves are filed in the album in classified, scientific order of the birds. This method brings together all the pictures of birds of one species and forms a picture book of bird families. Two indices are required, one by country to mark up what has been purchased, and a scientific index in the same order in which the album is arranged.

If a person is really interested in the bird depicted, however, this kind of collection, by random acquisition, soon seems to be lacking in purpose. An ornithologist will want an ornithological approach to the subject i.e. an arrangement not only bringing the birds together but one carried a stage further whereby a deeper knowledge of birds can be acquired and used. This can be achieved by selecting a certain group, or groups of birds for collecting.

Selective collecting has many advantages, and there is a wide choice of subjects. Basically these choices may be divided into two categories: 1. Geographically-based collections, and 2. Ornithologically-based collections, which are dealt with in the next three chapters. Being selective means that you can choose a group of countries or birds, and knowing in advance how many stamps are involved (retrospectively, at least), it is possible to make a fairly complete collection. If you envisage collecting for many years, then a largish group can be chosen, but if you prefer to have a small, more quickly assembled group, which you can then study in detail, that too is possible.

Your approach can be ecological, e.g. collect the birds of the tropics; or it can be zoogeographical, e.g. collect the birds of Australasia or Oriental species; or a favourite group of birds such as predators, ducks, waders. Such collections are manageable financially, fascinating to acquire and research, and give the collector time to learn about both the stamps and their artists as well as the birds depicted.

In the next three chapters I have suggested some suitable subjects, and worked out how many stamps would be involved for each subject, so that a prospective collector can have some idea as to what would be involved.

Books for comprehensive collections:

GIBBONS, S. *Stamps of the World.* A catalogue published annually.

GOODERS, J. *Birds: an illustrated survey of the bird families of the world.* 1975. Hamlyn.

GRUSON, E. S. *A Checklist of the birds of the world.* 1976. Collins.

STANLEY, W. F. *Birds of the world on stamps* (up to the end of 1972). 1974. Pubd America, available from British stamp shops.

3

Collecting bird stamps geographically

This is collecting on a regional basis, by country, by continent, or by some other method of dividing up the globe into smaller areas so that a collection of bird stamps illustrates the avifauna of that region.

No single country's output of bird stamps will give sufficient scope for a worthwhile collection since the most prolific postal authority, Cuba, has only issued just over 100 bird stamps. Those other countries which pour out pictorials are not usually the ones with either the best designs or most beautiful stamps. It is necessary therefore, to choose a bigger unit than a single country, or, should a collector be extremely interested in the bird species known to inhabit one country, he must then collect all the stamps depicting those species irrespective of which country (or postal authority) happens to have issued them.

The simplest method is to choose a region e.g. the British Commonwealth, and collect all the stamps issued by the countries in that region. Most of the stamps will depict Commonwealth birds, but a few rogues will appear in world-wide conservation sets, zoo sets, etc. The regional approach is already mapped out to a large extent by the Gibbons' stamp catalogues where the issues of the European countries (excluding their colonies), British Commonwealth, and Overseas (rest of the world and European colonies) are listed.

The arrangement of these collections may follow the arrangement in the Gibbons' catalogues, using the catalogue as an index by marking up what you have in stock, or making a personal index by extracting the appropriate entries from them. A more ambitious arrangement would be according to species of birds, requiring two indices—one by country and a classified list of bird species.

So far we have considered collecting within the confines of national or continental boundaries, the political boundaries imposed by man. Birds, however, ignore such artificial lines and have their own methods of recognising boundaries—physical ones like oceans, mountains and deserts. Zoologists have discovered which species of birds stay more or less within which natural boundaries and have, accordingly, divided the world into six regions. These are called zoo-geographical regions. Bird stamp collecting by these regions presents much more of a challenge and is consequently of greater interest. In addition, these regions form excellent bases for viable collections of bird stamps. Zoogeographical collecting will form the subject of Chapter 4.

Throughout the remainder of this chapter, Stanley's *Birds of the World on Stamps* and the Gibbons' catalogues will be the basic reference books for finding what bird stamps exist. Also, each time a figure is given for the number of bird stamps issued, it can be assumed that the number is a close approximation made from counting the stamps depicting clearly defined wild species of birds which form the main motif of the stamp or occupy at least half the surface area of the stamp. The counting was done to the end of 1974.

British Bird Stamps
Sadly, only 4 British birds have appeared on British stamps. These are the 4d Black-headed Gull, Blue Tit, Robin and Blackbird, issued as a set in 1966. We cannot count the 1963 4½d stamp since the three birds on this are so tiny, nor can we include the diminutive stylised owl of 1961 3d, nor the stylised swallows of the 1957 2½d World Scout Jubilee Jamboree. So if we wish to collect British birds on stamps we must look elsewhere.

In 1971 the British Ornithologists' Union issued a list of nearly 500 species of birds which had been seen in Britain

The only British bird set, 1966, all 4d, Robin, Blackbird, Black-headed Gull, Blue Tit, designed by J. Norris Wood.

and Ireland up to the end of 1970. Taking this list, *The Status of Birds in Britain and Ireland*, as a basis, the species listed therein can be checked against Stanley's list of bird stamps, and those stamps which illustrate members of our national bird list selected for purchase. The total is about 1,000 stamps showing very many attractive portraits of clearly recognisable species, though not all of the British species have yet appeared on stamps.

Any British bird-watcher will be familiar with a large number of these species, and for those he does not easily recognise as being British birds, there are numerous field-guides at reasonable prices, some of them no doubt already on his own book shelves. A small difficulty arises in that the names of the birds which the authors of these books have used vary, and for this reason it will be necessary to choose one English name, and stick to it. Names on the stamps themselves are sometimes misleading, inaccurate, and incorrectly spelled, and must not be considered in any way authoritative. Since the B.O.U. list is the official one, and likely to remain so for many years to come, and their terminology should be adopted for any writing you may do about your collection, it would be as well to purchase a copy and use that as your own standard list, adopting the English and scientific nomenclature.

Two other decisions will have to be made whilst collecting British birds on stamps. The first is whether to include all British birds regardless of which country issues them, or only from those countries where "our" birds spend part of their lives. To take an extreme example, if Cuba were to issue a stamp with a St Kilda Wren on it, would you purchase it? The second decision, is whether to include or exclude British local issues such as those of the islands of Carn Iar, Canna, Man, Jethou, Lundy, Sanda, St Kilda and Stroma (nearly 90 stamps). These stamps are used only within the islands concerned, or groups of islands, and any mail leaving the island for the mainland requires a British stamp. The local issues are very picturesque, but do not really qualify as stamps proper.

When writing up a collection of British stamps, notes can be made as to whether the species breeds or winters in each country and further background information can be added at will.

Some of Lundy's many Puffin local issues. 1929, 6p; 1957, 4p; 1962, 1p.

Books:

BRITISH ORNITHOLOGISTS' UNION, RECORDS COMMITTEE. *The Status of Birds in Britain & Ireland*; edited by D. W. Snow. 1971. Blackwell.

BRUUN, B. *The Hamlyn Guide to Birds of Britain and Europe.* 1972. Hamlyn.

HEINZEL, F. *et al The Birds of Britain and Europe.* 1972. Collins.

PETERSON, R. T. *et al Fieldguide to the Birds of Britain and Europe* (reprint). Collins.

Collecting European Bird Stamps

The Gibbons' catalogue in 3 volumes which deals with the stamps issued by European countries will be the reference book for this collection. Since this is a wide geographical area, many and varied will be the stamps and species in such a collection. It will include the Scandinavian stamps which are some of the most beautifully engraved bird stamps that have been issued, our own British stamps, and some of the most garish and poor quality stamps of the Eastern European countries. The communist bloc countries issue a lot of pictorials because they recognise that these stamps are a good source of revenue from collectors. By collecting their stamps, many colourful illustrations of birds could be acquired, but we should perhaps question whether their excessive postal zeal should be encouraged and whether we wish to buy cheap stamps from that source.

A complete collection of all bird stamps listed in Gibbons' European catalogue, would be relatively small, though extremely attractive. The statistics below demonstrate this:

All of Europe i.e. countries in Gibbons'
European Cat. 1975   565 bird stamps
of which Eastern Europe i.e. Albania, Bulgaria, Czech., East Germany, Hungary, Poland, Rumania, Russia, Yugoslavia   395 bird stamps

Note also, that a small proportion of the European bird stamps depict exotic birds to be found in the colonies of European countries. Collecting strictly what each country issued would thus give a collection of pictures of some of the species inhabiting Europe, plus a number of stamps depicting species from all over the world. One way to solve this dilemma would be to exclude the exotics, or, if they are thought to add colour and variety to the collection, their numbers could be increased by including European colonies' stamps taken from the Gibbons' Overseas catalogue. This would add a further 285 stamps.

If this collection appears too small, it could be enlarged by adopting the zoo-geographical region of which Europe forms a part—see Palaearctic Region on page 32. This is based on the area inhabited by "European" species which penetrate south of Europe as far as the Sahara and east of Europe (north of the Himalayas) as far as Japan.

Having acquired Gibbons' European catalogue little further paper work will be required. A map showing the area it is proposed to cover would assist in keeping boundaries in mind, and show at a glance what has been included and excluded. The album would be arranged by countries within the scheme. The field-guides to the birds of Britain and Europe give illustrations of the European species, but if the exotic species from colonies are included in the collection, then their illustrations will have to be sought in numerous other books depicting other countries' avifauna.

Books:
GIBBONS, S. *Europe—Stamp catalogues.* 3 vols (A–F; G–P; Q–Z). Kept up to date but pubd irregularly.
VOOUS, K. H. *Atlas of European Birds.* 1960. Nelson.

Collecting British Commonwealth Bird Stamps
Collecting Commonwealth stamps of all descriptions has been a favourite pursuit of a great many philatelists for over a century, and because of them, Commonwealth stamps have been preserved in numbers. This gives a British collector a great advantage, since they are in plentiful supply, and reasonably priced with few exceptions. There is plenty of scope for a collection of the bird stamps from Commonwealth countries, since there are 900 stamps which qualify from 80 postal authorities, counting those listed in the *British Commonwealth Stamp Catalogue* up to the end of 1974.

Since the countries involved are in nearly every part of the globe, the birds form a splendidly varied collection, from the penguins of Antarctica to tropical species, hummingbirds of the West Indies and ocean birds which nest on islands in remote seas. The collection would include classic stamps and modern pictorials, the standard of which will be high because those countries which issue poor quality stamps (Middle East, some South American and some from the eastern bloc of Europe) are naturally excluded.

Papua & New Guinea

Bird stamps arranged geographically by country. Some of the stamps issued by Papua & New Guinea.

Finding the pictures in books of the bird species illustrated on the stamps for identification purposes will prove a laborious task. This can be avoided by accepting Stanley's identifications in *Birds of the World on Stamps.*

A Commonwealth bird stamp collection would be arranged under the country of issue. Arranging the stamps by bird species is hardly worth the labour involved, because the species depicted represent only a tiny fraction of the number of birds which choose to inhabit Her Majesty's dominions, and there will be few families even which will be fully represented by Commonwealth birds on stamps.

A decision as to whether to collect the stamps of countries which have been granted their independence, after Independence Day, or whether to stop collecting their stamps from the day they left the Commonwealth, will have to be made in the early stages of collecting. The current British Commonwealth catalogue of Gibbons includes post independent issues of Ireland, Pakistan, Rhodesia and South Africa. Adding these to your collection will enlarge it only very slightly at the moment, but who knows what will happen in the future?

Books:

GIBBONS, S. *British Commonwealth Stamp Catalogue.* Pubd annually.

STATESMAN'S YEARBOOK. Macmillan. Pubd annually.

A YEARBOOK OF THE COMMONWEALTH H.M.S.O. Pubd annually.

Overseas

Gibbons issues another stamp catalogue, which covers the countries outside Europe and the British Commonwealth. Many interesting and beautiful bird stamps are issued by these countries and some collections could be formed by grouping countries according to one's own interests. The following list might suggest some collections which could be formed from the stamps listed in the *Overseas Stamp Catalogue.*

Africa (north of the Sahara 40, south of the Sahara 700)	740	stamps depicting birds
N. America, Canada and Islands	50	stamps depicting birds
Central America	130	stamps depicting birds
South America	290	stamps depicting birds
Islands off S. America	100+	stamps depicting birds
Cuba	100+	stamps depicting birds
India and the Far East	180	stamps depicting birds

However, there are so many other collections which may be formed, and which are outlined in the following pages, that I have left the rest of the Overseas catalogue for anyone who wishes to explore its possibilities for himself.

Book:

GIBBONS, S. *Overseas stamp catalogues.* 4 vols (A–C; D–J; K–O; P–Z). Pubd irreg.

4

Collecting Bird Stamps
Zoo-geographically

Scientists have discovered that the geographical distribution of birds is determined by factors which set limits to their range, such as climate and its effect on the terrain (e.g. high rainfall results in tropical forests and lack of rainfall produces desert regions), and land masses (divided by oceans and mountain ranges). Since birds are capable of flying long distances, there are some species which cross such barriers as mountains and oceans, and these may winter in one region and breed in another, but on the whole, the physical barriers do act as boundaries for more sedentary species. The six regions into which the world has been divided (see map facing) are therefore guide-line divisions convenient for studying the avifauna inhabiting certain kinds of terrain under given climatic conditions—and they also form convenient groups for interesting bird stamp collections. The regions are broader divisions than countries and therefore offer more variety of species and more stamps to collect, yet they are within manageable collecting proportions. We shall take them one at a time and see what is available within each of the six regions and try to assess how good a collection of stamps could be formed for each.

Arranging a zoo-geographical collection of bird stamps
The bird stamps of a zoo-geographical region would be arranged by the names of the species of birds inhabiting that region. This requires either finding or making a list of the species of the region's avifauna, and then checking this list

30

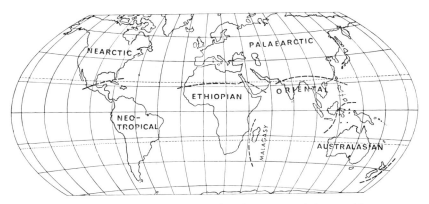

Map showing zoo-geographical regions of the world.

against the scientifically arranged index of species whose portraits have appeared on stamps in W. F. Stanley's *Birds of the World on Stamps*. Those species which have been depicted will be noted, and the list will include stamps from all postal authorities, either within or without the region. The reason for there being some issuing authorities outside the boundaries of your region is that some bird species are to be found in a number of zoo-geographical regions. For example, a collector of Nearctic (N. American) species would want all the stamps depicting the Swallow *Hirundo rustica* whether issued by European, South African, Australian, Argentine or Ceylon postal authorities. The arrangement of the album will follow the scientific listing of the species, under their scientific names.

It would be helpful to draw up a large map with the boundaries clearly marked and the names of the postal authorities and countries within the region written inside the boundaries in their appropriate places. It is a good idea, also, to write a list of the names of countries which are no longer used, by the side of the map (especially for the Ethiopian, or African Region).

Book:
GRUSON, E. S. *A Checklist of the Birds of the World*. 1976. Collins (Gives distribution of each species).

Collecting Birds of the Palaearctic Region on Stamps

1,380 Stamps

Birds of the Palaearctic Region are to be found within the western boundaries of the Atlantic, west of Iceland; the southern boundaries of the Sahara in Africa and the Himalayas in Asia; and the eastern boundary of the Pacific Ocean, east of Japan.

This may be a vast area to cover, but it has the distinct advantage of including our own British birds, and therefore a nucleus of species with which we are familiar. In addition, many field-guides with adequate illustrations of the birds of Europe are available for identifying the species depicted on the stamps. We also have a complete list of the birds of the Palaearctic avifauna which can be used to check which species are included in this region. This is the two volume work by Vaurie.

Collecting bird stamps of the Palaearctic region would reveal many interesting facts about the birds' distribution and choice of habitat within the region. Some pictures of a species might show it in winter plumage, whilst others include a drawing of the nest and eggs of that species, depending on which country issues the stamps and whether the artist sees the bird in its winter quarters or the breeding part of its range. Discovering where "our" birds fly to, during their migrations, is another interesting aspect.

Up to the end of 1974 some 1,380 stamps had been issued with pictures of the birds of the Palaearctic region. Most of these stamps were issued by European countries (565 stamps), North Africa and the Middle East (400 stamps), and Asia (140 stamps) making a total of 1,105 stamps. The remainder were issued by countries in other zoo-geographical regions which share some of our species of birds. Among these are some warblers which spend their winter in South Africa in the Ethiopian Region, and some divers, grebes, ducks, etc. which also inhabit the Nearctic Region, and so on.

Many of the Middle East countries have issued far too many cheap stamps. Gibbons has placed some of them, mainly from the Persian Gulf area, in their Appendix to the

Birds of the Palaearctic avifauna.

annual *Stamps of the World* catalogue. A collector of this region would have to decide whether or not to include Appendix items. These troublesome issues could be avoided if one were to adopt a new book, now being published, as the basis of the collection. Stanley Cramp and collaborators are compiling a seven volume exhaustive study of the birds of the western Palaearctic fauna, which will cover all Europe west of Russia, east to Turkey and Jordan, and south to about 20°N in Africa. Collecting the stamps depicting the species and subspecies in this book would restrict the collection to the better quality Palaearctic bird stamps and make the collection of more manageable proportions.

Birds of the Palaearctic Region. Hungary 1973 Wren; Japan 1963/4 Ptarmigan; Iceland 1967 Great Northern Diver; Czechoslovakia 1960 Great Crested Grebe.

Books:

CRAMP, S. *et al. The Birds of the Western Palearctic.* 7 vols, vol. 1 1977. Oxford University Press.

ETCHÉCOPAR, R. D. & HUÉ, P. *The Birds of North Africa.* 1967. Oliver & Boyd.

VAURIE, C. *The Birds of the Palearctic Fauna.* 2 vols. 1959–1963. H. F. & G. Witherby. (Out of print.)

General Reference:
THE MIDDLE EAST AND NORTH AFRICA (an annual survey and
reference book). Pubd annually. Europa Pubns.
THE EUROPA YEAR BOOK 1975: A WORLD SURVEY. Vol. 1. *Inter-
national organisations, Europe.* Europa Pubns Vol. 2.
Africa, the Americas, Asia, Australasia. Europa Pubns.
Pubd annually.

Collecting Birds of the Nearctic Region on Stamps

550 Stamps

Strange as it may seem, the postal authorities of this vast
area have produced very few bird stamps—only about 50.
This is because the countries or states involved, U.S.A.,
Canada, Newfoundland and St Pierre & Miquelon, have
been so reticent in their postal issuing policy. Therefore a
collector wishing to take an interest in North American bird
species depicted on stamps will have little option other than
to adopt the policy of collecting birds of the Nearctic Region
on stamps irrespective of their source of issue.

Scientists call the area of North America, north of the
tropics, the Nearctic Region. The southern boundary line
passes through Mexico, the northern boundary being the
Arctic Ocean. There are so many species closely related to
those of the Palaearctic avifauna that sometimes the birds of
the Nearctic Region are joined with those of the Palaearctic
Region and together form a larger area referred to as the
Holarctic Region. This larger area could be of use to a bird
stamp collector who would thereby form a collection of the
birds of the northern hemisphere on stamps.

Apart from some typical northern hemisphere species of
birds, the Nearctic avifauna includes more colourful exotic
species from the southern states, such as motmots. Also a
number of North American species winter in the warmer
climate of the Central and South American countries, so that
the list of stamps whose birds illustrate Nearctic species will
include a number of South American countries' bird stamps.
Similarly, some members of the Nearctic avifauna also occur
on the eastern side of the Atlantic and form part of the
Palaearctic avifauna. Thus, the stamps which illustrate the

birds of the Nearctic avifauna will be collected from many countries outside the boundaries of North America and Canada:

North American countries illustrating
 Nearctic birds   — 50 stamps
Other countries illustrating Nearctic
birds   —500 stamps
Total number of Nearctic birds on stamps   =550 stamps

What is to be done about Greenland, is the one small problem in this region. The scientists recognise that it should be included in the Nearctic Region with North America, but most of the birds in Greenland are distinctly European, i.e. Palaearctic in character. The only genuinely wild bird species depicted on a Greenland stamp so far, was issued for that country by Denmark in 1945 (twice, both 5k values) and showed a beautifully drawn Eider Duck. Since the Eider is part of both avifaunas, no problem arises over that, but any new issues might well pose a difficulty in future.

The northern birds are numerous, both sea and land species, with many ducks which are so attractive on stamps, and divers, grebes, and game birds. Though not so glamorous as African, South American and Australasian birds, the wealth of different species offers the opportunity to form an attractive collection.

Birds of the Nearctic Region. St Pierre & Miquelon 1963 Ringed Plovers; Canada 1969 10c Ipswich Sparrow; Canada 1969 25c Hermit Thrush; U.S.A. 1967 Collie's Magpie-Jay.

Books:

AMERICAN ORNITHOLOGISTS' UNION. *Checklist of North Ameri-*
can Birds. A.O.U. 1957.

GODFREY, W. E. *The Birds of Canada.* 1974. (Pubd Ottawa).

ROBBINS, C. S. *et al Birds of North America* (identification
guide). 1966.

American stamp catalogue:

SCOTT PUB. CO. *Standard Stamp Catalogue.* Vol. 1. *U.S. and*
affiliated Territories. Annual.

Collecting Birds of the Neotropical Region on Stamps

860 Stamps

This region's avifauna is the richest in the world and has
some unique forms such as rheas, screamers, the hoatzin,
trumpeters, sunbitterns, seed-snipes, potoos and oilbirds.
Apart from these curious species, there are multitudes of
brilliantly-plumaged birds which live in the tropical rain
forests.

The region is comprised of tropical North America (south
from the northern edge of the tropical rain forests of
Mexico), Central America and South America, together with
the West Indies and the islands off South America. If all the
stamps which illustrate Neotropical species are collected,
irrespective of the source of issue (i.e. postal authorities both
within and without the South American continent) then a
collection of 860 stamps would result.

The Neotropical Region is, in fact, one of the best regions
to choose from the point of view of the wonderful range of
bird species, number of stamps, and the possibility of adding
to the size of the collection, or reducing it (e.g. by omitting
islands) to suit any collector's interests.

One small decision over exclusion or inclusion would have
to be made with regard to an item in Gibbons' Appendix,
1976. This concerns the Paraguay stamps issued since 1962.
Before 1962 Paraguay had issued only 3 bird stamps and
these are listed in the main body of the *Stamps of the World*

Stamps with clear, well-centred pictures of birds.

catalogue, but since 1966, 22 more bird stamps have been issued and placed in the Appendix. These well designed and most attractive stamps include some reproductions of A. Singer's illustrations from O. L. Austin's book *Birds of the World*, and it would be a pity to forego collecting them. Since the number is so small, an exception to the rule not to include Appendix items could perhaps be made in this case.

Books:

BARBOUR, T. *Cuban ornithology.* 1943 (only 2 plates).

DAVIS, L. I. *A Fieldguide to the Birds of Mexico and Central America.* 1972. Univ. Texas.

PETERSON, R. T. & CHALIF, E. L. *A field-guide to Mexican Birds (including Guatemala, British Honduras, El Salvador).* 1973.

SCHAUENSEE, R. M. de *Guide to the Birds of South America.* 1971. (Livingstone, Pa.).

THE EUROPA YEAR BOOK: A WORLD SURVEY *see* Vol. 2. *Africa, the Americas, Asia, Australasia* (June 1975. 26th ed).

Birds of the Neotropical Region. Guyana 1968 Hoatzin; Ecuador 1966 Pavonine Quetzal; Cuba 1967 Sulphur-breasted Toucan; Argentine 1967 Amazon Kingfisher; Panama 1967 Turquoise-browed Motmot; Peru 1972 Andean Cock-of-the-Rock.

Collecting Birds of the Ethiopian Region   1,175 Stamps
This group of birds has its attractions in that Africa is the
wintering place of many of our own familiar species, and it
also provides some exotic birds, as one would expect from an
area which includes both the equator and the Tropics of
Capricorn and Cancer. A region with barbets, weavers, and
parrots, as well as the curious Secretary Bird and Hammer-
head, pretty little mousebirds and stately Crowned Cranes,
certainly has a lot to offer. However, collecting African
birds on stamps is not as simple as it sounds.

The scientists who have studied the avifauna of the
African continent have discovered that the Sahara Desert
forms a natural barrier which most species living in southern
Africa do not cross. For this reason, only Africa south of a
line drawn beneath the Sahara Desert, and extending east to
cut off a small south-western portion of Arabia, is included
in the region they call Ethiopian. The northern part of Africa
thus separated by this line, is included in the Palaearctic
Region in which the birds are the same as, or very closely
related to, our British and other European species.

This division poses a number of alternatives for the collector of African bird stamps. It is necessary first of all to
define the area whose species are to be collected. Is it to be
the whole of the African continent, or the Ethiopian region?
The following figures might assist that decision.
Bird stamps issued by African countries
    (a) North of the Sahara 40
    (b) South of the Sahara 700
Bird stamps depicting the Avifauna of the Ethiopian
    Region 1,175

If the Ethiopian Region is chosen, two small decisions
about the inclusion or exclusion of stamps will have to be
made. The first concerns the stamps from the states situated
in the south-western portion of the Arabian Peninsula viz.
Yemen. Yemen had issued stamps from 1926, but following
a revolt in 1962 both a Royalist and a Republican government issued stamps until 1970. On 23rd July 1970 Saudi
Arabia transferred its support from the Royalist government
(set up in 1962), to the unified government of the Yemen

Republic, and Saudi Arabian mail transit facilities were withdrawn from the Royalist (Mutawakelite) Kingdom. It is doubtful if supplies of new issues from the Royal Yemen after 1970 were actually used. An added complication occurred in 1967 when Gibbons decided that both parts of the Yemen were issuing too many stamps and removed them both to the Appendix! Unfortunately, quite a number of bird stamps is involved in this saga. I list the bird stamps of the Yemen below, so that a collector can decide for himself what to include and exclude.

Yemen 1926–1962 issued	No bird stamps
Yemen Republic 1962–67 (in main body of Gibbons' Cat.)	14 bird stamps
Yemen Royalist 1962–67 (in main body of Gibbons' Cat.)	12 bird stamps
Yemen Royalist 1967–July 1970 (In Gibbons' Appendix)	7 bird stamps
Yemen Republic 1967–July 1970	No bird stamps
Yemen People's Democratic Republic 1970–	4 bird stamps

(There are also five Royalist stamps, issued in 1971, of considerable doubt as to their authenticity.)

The second point to consider is the large island of Madagascar (from 14th October 1958 the Malagasy Republic). This is sometimes considered as a separate region from the Ethiopian Region, because as large a number as 118 of its known 200 species are found nowhere else in the world. For our purposes, however, it can be included in the Ethiopian Region—only 9 stamps are involved anyway.

Anyone collecting African stamps needs a good deal of patience in dealing with the numerous changes of name which occurred when countries became independent, or divided to form new states. Fortunately this vexed question has been well documented and explained for stamp collectors in four articles by H. D. Black, called "Whatever happened to Africa", and published in the Stanley Gibbons' journal *Stamp Monthly* in the months August, September, November 1971 and January 1972. A further source for current data on these countries, under their modern names, is *Africa South of the Sahara*, Europa Publications, which is an annual survey and reference book.

Books:

BANNERMAN, D. A. *Birds of West & Equatorial Africa*. 2 vols. 1951–3. Oliver & Boyd.

MACKWORTH-PRAED. C. W. & GRANT, C. H. B. *African Handbook of Birds*. 6 vols. 1952–73. Longmans.

Series 1. *Birds of Eastern & North-western Africa*. 2 vols.

Series 2. *Birds of the southern third of Africa*. 2 vols.

Series 3. *Birds of West Central & Western Africa*. 2 vols.

PROZESKY, O. P. M. *A Field-guide to the birds of Southern Africa*. 1974. Collins.

Birds of the Ethiopian Region. Lesotho 1971 Ground Woodpecker; Swaziland 1968 Long-tailed Widow-bird; Bechuanaland 1961 Swallow-tailed Bee-eater; Uganda 1965 Lilac-breasted Roller; The Gambia 1966 Golden Bishop; Cameroon 1962 Ostrich; Sudan 1951 Whale-headed Stork.

Collecting birds of the Oriental Region   1,000 Stamps
The boundaries of this area, the Oriental Region, are south
of a line running through the Himalayas, east to include
Yunnan and Szechwan, and south to include Sri Lanka
(Ceylon), Sumatra, Timor, and the Philippine Islands, with
Taiwan (Formosa) at the north-east boundary. 1,000 stamps
have been issued with pictures of the species of the Oriental
avifauna.

These stamps require a great deal of patience to assemble,
and some would be extremely difficult to obtain. Neverthe-
less, the birds depicted will compensate for the difficulties in
finding the stamps. Some have enchanting names like
laughing thrushes, and fairy blue birds, and there are
wonderfully colourful pittas, pastel-shaded white-eyes and
the unlikely-sounding Red-whiskered Bulbul. More familiar,
because they are favourite cage-birds in Britain, are the
talking mynahs. There are also a few parrots, some gro-
tesque hornbills, cheerful little trogons and many kinds of
woodpecker and honeyeater.

One set of stamps which will pose a problem, because it is
listed in Gibbons' Appendix, will be the beautiful issue from
Ajman in 1971 which reproduced 16 of the charming illustrations from John Gould's *Birds of Asia* (published in 7 vols.
1850–1883, with 520 plates). The stamps are so attractive
that they are hard to resist.

Illustrations of the birds and lists of the bird species of the
Oriental Region have to be sought in a number of books
since no single title includes all of them. This, plus the difficulty in obtaining some of the stamps, would make the
collecting of this group a formidable task.

Books:
DELACOUR, J. & MAYR, E. *The Birds of the Philippines.* 1946
(New York).
MEDWAY, LORD and WELLS, DAVID R. *The Birds of the Malay
Peninsula, Vol 5.* 1976. H. F. & G. Witherby.
KING, B. *et al A Field-guide to the Birds of South East Asia.*
1975. Collins. (Every known species of Burma, Malaya,
Thailand, Cambodia, Vietnam, Laos, Hong Kong,

Taiwan incl. illus. of 1,157 birds.)

RIPLEY, S. D. *A Synopsis of the birds of India & Pakistan, together with those of Nepal, Sikkim, Bhutan and Ceylon.* 1961. (Bombay.)

For background information:

THE FAR EAST & AUSTRALASIA Europa Pubns. Pubd annually.

Birds of the Oriental Region. Bhutan 1968 Crimson-winged Laughing Thrush; Ceylon 1966 Peacock; Singapore 1963 White-breasted Kingfisher; Burma 1964 Indian Roller; India 1975 Indian Pitta; Malaysia 1965 Rhinoceros Hornbill; North Viet-Nam 1973 Collared Fantails.

Collecting birds of the Australasian Region   850 Stamps
Ever since the first explorers went to New Holland, as
Australia was originally called, and returned home with tales
of Black Swans, the birds of this region have been a source of
wonder and amazement. During the last two hundred years,
scientists have discovered and described about 650 species
seen in Australia. The birds include such strange and beautiful species as Kookaburras, Lyrebirds, bower birds, brilliant
Blue Wrens, cockatoos, and many others. They all add up to
a galaxy of unusual species in a land where natural greeny-
yellow budgerigars gather in flocks at waterholes.

However, this is not the only country with many unique
birds in this region. New Zealand has produced a number of
attractive stamps to show the rest of the world how beautiful, and sometimes strange, are her bird species—especially
the Kiwi. New Guinea birds also form part of the avifauna of
the region, with species to be found in Papua, New Hebrides,
Niue and Penrhyn Island, not forgetting the Kagus from
New Caledonia and its dependency Wallis & Futuna Islands,
which have appeared on over 50 stamps. From a philatelist's
and a birdman's point of view, there seems to be everything
one could wish for in a collection of the bird stamps depicting the avifauna of the Australasian Region.

The stamps themselves are as varied as the birds, from the
classical Black Swans of Western Australia to the very elegant modern reproductions of Gregory Mathews' birds of
Norfolk Island (issued as a definitive set in 1970). Unfortunately, because this collection includes very early Commonwealth material, it would be an extremely expensive collection to bring together. To acquire all of the 300 stamps issued
by the postal authorities within the region would be too
costly an undertaking for most collectors. The mint stamps
depicting Black Swans (of Western Australia) alone would
be anyway virtually unobtainable. This need not deter since it
would be possible to collect bird stamps issued only by
current postal authorities—so cutting out Western Australia
and Wallis & Futuna Islands. Variations on this idea could
be costed and I have no doubt some satisfactory solutions
would emerge.

Books:

ANNOTATED CHECKLIST OF THE BIRDS OF NEW ZEALAND including the birds of the Ross Dependency. 1970 (N.Z.).

FALLA, R. A. *et al Birds of New Zealand.* 2 vols. 1966. Collins reprint 1975.

IREDALE, T. *Birds of New Guinea.* 2 vols. 1956 (Melbourne).

MACDONALD, J. D. *Birds of Australia.* 1973. H. F. & G. Witherby.

RAND, A. L. & GILLIARD, T. E. *Handbook of New Guinea Birds.* 1967. Weidenfeld & Nicolson.

SLATER, P. *A Field-guide to Australian Birds.* Vol. 1. *Non-Passerine* 1972. Vol. 2. *Passerines* 1975. Oliver & Boyd.

For background information:

THE FAR EAST & AUSTRALASIA Europa Pubns. Pubd annually.

Birds of the Australasian Region. Papua, New Guinea 1973 Queen Carola's Bird of Paradise; Niue 1971 Polynesian Triller; Norfolk Is. 1970 Norfolk Island Pigeon (ext); Australia 1954 Black Swan; New Zealand 1956 Takahe; Australia 1964 Scarlet Robin.

Collecting Island birds on stamps

Perhaps it is because we live on a large, very overcrowded island ourselves that other small but less densely populated islands are so attractive to us. Collecting island bird stamps is a most appealing idea, and since many of the world's islands come under British jurisdiction, or did at one time in their history, their stamps are relatively easy to find and purchase in Britain.

The following groups are made up mainly from islands not included in the zoo-geographical regions. Those already included in those regions could be added to these to make a fascinating island bird stamp collection, though defining "island" might prove difficult. Perhaps a size limit should be imposed, otherwise Great Britain, New Zealand and Japan will creep in and spoil the pleasant "away from it all" atmosphere of a small island collection.

It would be easier to collect the stamps issued by these islands, rather than attempt to list all the species known to visit the islands, and collect stamps depicting those species whatever their source. So we shall proceed along these lines, and look at what bird stamps have been issued by island postal authorities.

The **Atlantic Islands**, St Helena, Fernando Poo, Tristan da Cunha, South Georgia, Ascension Island and the Falkland Islands, have nearly 50 stamps between them, which include some outstanding sets. Some sea-bird species are familiar, whilst the island forms of the land birds indicate some fascinating specialisation to adapt them to life on stormy islands with a limited variety of food.

Going through the **Mediterranean** on our way to the east, we find just two islands with bird stamps—Cyprus which has 5 stamps, and Malta with 2 stamps.

The **Indian Ocean** offers some different species which prefer warmer climes. Between them the Seychelles, Mauritius, Christmas Island, Cocos (Keeling) Is., Comoro Is., Maldive Is., and the British Indian Ocean Territory, have over 80 stamps illustrating some very rare bird species. We might add Malagasy Republic, the old Madagascar, whose 9 bird stamps include some of its unique avifauna.

The **Pacific Ocean** has many islands which fit the picture of ideal places for the castaway. They have a greater variety of bird-life too, and over 90 stamps illustrate these, mainly pelagic species. They come from Samoa, Tonga, Pitcairn, Aitutaki, British Solomon Islands, Cook Island, Fiji, French (Oceanic Settlements) Polynesia, Gilbert & Ellice Is., and Nauru. Again, some lovely sets are included in these stamps for it would seem there is something about the free wanderers of the oceans which has inspired artists and designers to their best efforts.

Our last group of islands is the largest and has many British possessions amongst its number—the **West Indies** and nearby islands in the West Atlantic. Perhaps these should be with the other Atlantic Islands for a neater geographic arrangement, but the West Indies conjure up visions of warm beaches and humming birds, whilst the other Atlantic Islands are distinctly chilly. Anguilla, the Bahamas, Bermuda, Cayman Islands, Dominica, Grenada, Haiti, Jamaica, Montserrat, St Christopher, St Lucia, St Vincent, Trinidad & Tobago, Turks & Caicos, and the Virgin Islands account for about 140 bird stamps. These depict flamingoes, tropic birds, frigate birds, pelicans, bananaquits, parrots unique to St Lucia and St Vincent, and some pretty pigeons. There is just one difficult question to settle—what to do with Cuba? We cannot deny its island status but its stamps are troublesome. Cuba issues far too many bird stamps with the sole object of persuading collectors, that is us, to help fill Castro's coffers. We could buy over 100 of Cuba's stamps (about a dozen of which do not depict Cuban birds) and the question is—do we want to?

Without Cuba, a complete island collection, as outlined above, would give a group of some 400 stamps of good quality, including some well-produced and designed single issues and some delightful sets. The collection could be expanded by adding in other islands not listed above, and gives plenty of scope for imaginative grouping and selecting. Turning the pages of an album of island birds would be like setting out on a voyage of ornithological discovery, perhaps

Island bird stamps.

accompanying Captain Cook, but without the discomforts of life on board ship 200 years ago.

Books:

BANNERMAN, D. A. *Birds of the Atlantic Islands.* 4 vols. 1963–71.

BELCHER, W. J. & GIBSON, R. B. *Birds of Fiji in colour.* 1973. Collins.

BOND, J. *Birds of the West Indies.* 1974 (1st ed 1960). Collins.

BRUDENELL-BRUCE, P. G. C. *Birds of New Providence and the Bahama Islands.* 1975. Collins.

PENNY, M. *The Birds of the Seychelles.* 1975. Collins.

Summary of Bird Stamp Collections outlined in
Chapters 3 and 4

Geographical Region	No. of bird stamps issued by countries in that region
Britain	4 (But there are 1,000 stamps issued by other postal authorities which illustrate British bird species)
Europe	565
+ European Colonies	+285
N. America, Canada & Islands	50
S. America, Central America	620
The Americas (N. & S. islands)	670
The African Continent	740
Middle East	400
India & Far East	180
Australia, New Zealand, New Guinea	300
British Commonwealth	900
The World's Islands	400

Zoo-geographical Region	No. of stamps issued by any postal authority depicting species of the avifauna of that region
Palaearctic Region	1,380 (1,100 were issued by the countries within the Pal. region)
Nearctic Region	550
Holarctic Region	1,550
Neotropical Region	860
Ethiopian Region	1,175
Oriental Region	1,000
Australasian Region	850

5

Collecting Bird Stamps Ornithologically

A bird-watcher in Britain has nearly 500 species of which he might be fortunate enough to see a great many in his career. Coming to terms with these species and learning to identify them in the field takes years of patient endeavour. The thought of learning what the other known 8,100 species of birds look like, and where they are to be found, is so daunting that one might be forgiven for despairing of such an achievement. Through bird stamp collecting, however, it is possible to gradually and painlessly come to recognise first a few, then more, and finally hundreds of foreign species. By arranging the bird stamps scientifically, a detailed knowledge of the organisation and structure of the bird world may be acquired.

The usual approach to bird stamp collecting is through an interest in the birds, their physical appearance and world distribution, rather than an interest in the stamps, though the finer points of philately often come to be appreciated later. The conventional arrangement of stamps in an album is under the names of countries, but, since it is the birds which claim our interest, it is logical to arrange the album in the scientific order of the birds. However, it is likely to be too large an undertaking for anyone to collect all the bird stamps available and arrange them scientifically, so some selection is necessary. Collecting ornithologically means that we select the stamps which illustrate certain groups of birds, such as Sea Birds, Wildfowl, or Birds of Prey, and arrange them scientifically. The scientific classification of *Aves* organises birds with similar characteristics into groups, so that species which are very similar in character are collected together in a genus; similar genera are placed in one Family; Families with affinities are grouped in an Order. All the birds are included in 28 Orders, and these are useful divisions for us as bird stamp collectors.

The advantage to collecting groups of birds, perhaps favourite kinds such as predators, or parrots, is that our knowledge of the birds is increased at the same time as our knowledge of their distribution. Concentrating on one carefully selected group, gives one the chance to complete, or almost complete a collection, leaving some spare time to read about the species illustrated. Knowing what is involved in collecting bird stamps illustrating the species of a single Order, it is possible either to restrict the collection to that Order, or to expand it by adding other closely associated Families to form a special combination giving the collector a unique collection of his own devising.

The disadvantages to collecting ornithologically arise mainly because sets of bird stamps rarely depict only species from a single Order or Family of birds. Just a small proportion of sets are of birds of prey, or pheasants, or parrots, etc., most are a colourful mixture of different types of birds. This means that sets have to be split up and some unwanted stamps disposed of—a tricky proposition because the trade dislikes incomplete sets. If you are a member of a club, another collector might cooperate by relieving you of unwanted stamps. It is easier to obtain odd stamps from a set in the used condition, rather than mint, so this type of collecting suggests you might choose to buy only used stamps. Setenant stamps will have to be separated, and there is another problem when two, three, or even more species are depicted on the one stamp. The three macaws on the French Guinea 1947 25f and 40f, also the four toucans on the 200f can be accommodated on a separate album leaf just before or after the parrot and toucan sections in your album, and be indexed in the classified list of stamps. The 8-bird stamp of Poland 1966 10gr covered a number of Families in the large Order *Passeriformes*, and would be difficult to place. However,

some solutions will occur to you when you come across these
problems. As long as the species are referred to in the index
they are not lost. Omitting them from the collection altogether is not a good solution, because you sacrifice variety by
such exclusions.

*Composite Bird Stamps. Maldive Is. 1968 Curlew & Red-
shank; Poland 1966 Jay, Green Woodpecker, Golden
Oriole, Redstart, Great Tit, Hoopoe, Chaffinch, Siskin;
Dominica 1970 Imperial and Red-necked Parrots.*

Arranging stamps ornithologically

Since the interest in collecting ornithologically is mostly in
the birds and only partly in the stamps, it is reasonable to
also arrange the stamps ornithologically i.e. in a classified
scientific order. Every bird book you consult will differ
slightly in both the scientific names allotted to the species
and in the sequence in which the species are listed. There is
no need to worry about this. Treat the names as "handles"
only, and if you adopt one list which includes all the bird
species in which you are interested, and use that author's
choice and sequence of bird names, repeating them in your
own personal catalogue of stamps, and the classified index to

it, then no muddle will ensue. It is wise to keep the name simple, i.e. adopt the two names which form the species name (the binomial). Those birds which have been given three names (a trinomial or subspecies name) differ only slightly in physique from the other birds bearing the first two of those three names, and you can safely ignore the third name. For example, *Egretta alba* is the Great White Heron. The Great White Heron of Comores *Egretta alba melanorhynchos* differs only slightly from the Great White Heron of New Zealand *Egretta alba modesta*—and on the stamps concerned the difference can certainly not be detected. Some collectors might like to use the subspecies trinomial to distinguish those birds which are island forms, and keen ornithologists may enjoy working out which subspecies is likely to be illustrated, but using subspecies' names creates a great deal of extra work for very little return in terms of bird stamp collecting.

If you are so fortunate as to have a modern monograph on the birds which are the subject of your collection, then you will already have used it to identify each species and find the information about its life history, distribution, and a picture of it for comparison with the stamp design of the bird. It would seem sensible then to adopt the author's classification and keep to that, rather than search for other authors' ideas on the classification of your group and so become confused.

There may be no single outstanding monograph containing a classification guide for your particular birds. In that case, the general guides listed at the end of this section will be of use.

One other point to bear in mind—any name in any language printed on the stamp itself or in printed catalogues must be treated with the utmost caution, even scepticism, for they are frequently incorrect.

You will most probably have made out a list of the bird stamps you own, and the ones you wish to purchase, under the names of the countries issuing them. A second list should be made which will be in the same order in which the stamps themselves appear in the album. For example, if you collect the Crane Order i.e. Gruiformes, then the classified index would look like the following extract, and the pages in the album would be headed like the example illustrated opposite.

Order GRUIFORMES
  Family GRUIDAE
    Genus GRUS

Crane (Eurasian)	Grus grus	Afghanistan 1974
		Finland 1951
		Germany DR 1967
		Roumania 1965
		Sweden 1968
		Yugoslavia 1958
Whooping Crane	Grus americana	Canada 1955
		U.S.A. 1957

    Genus ANTHROPOIDES

Blue or Stanley Crane	Anthropoides paradisea	S. Africa 1974

    Genus BALEARICA

Crowned Crane	Balearica pavonina	Bulgaria 1968
		Burundi 1965; 1967; 1970
		Cameroun 1971
		Congo (Braz.) 1967
		Congo (Leo.) 1963
		Cuba 1967
		Ghana 1959
		etc. etc.

It may sound extravagant, but I strongly recommend never putting more than one species on an album leaf. This will prove more economical in the long run, because if you crowd your stamps initially, you will have to remount them at a later date. This re-mounting means extra time, extra handling, new sheets to be purchased and new hinges. I allotted just sufficient space for one Purple-throated Carib, when first arranging my album. After all, up to 1968 only one had been issued in 118 years. Who would have guessed that in the next two years five more Purple-throated Caribs would appear? They did, and I had to give them a new sheet to themselves thereby making myself a lot of extra work.

Flexibility in mounting and generous spacing are both essential, if an expanding collection is envisaged. If you work within set date-lines, then more precise spacing can be

Order   GRUIFORMES
Family   GRUIDAE
Genus   BALEARICA
Species *Balearica pavonina*   Crowned Crane

*Stamps arranged ornithologically by the scientific order
of bird species. Crowned Cranes Balearica pavonina.*

calculated. This sort of collecting, however, is far less fun, and most of us prefer to keep up with new issues and enjoy seeing newly created designs. Hence the need to leave room for newcomers.

Books:
For the standard reference books for special subjects see under the subject sections.

GRUSON, E. S. *A Checklist of the Birds of the World.* 1976. Collins.

PETERS, J. L. *Checklist of the Birds of the World.* Vols. 1–15 (8 & 11 not yet published). 1931– Unavailable outside reference libraries and too detailed for most people.

STANLEY, W. F. *Birds of the World on Stamps.* 1974.

We can now consider some different groups which would form attractive collections.

Collecting Sea-birds on stamps
This topic would be most useful for a beginner, because it could be of narrow definition initially and expanded later on. Most of the sea-going birds, the gulls, terns, waders, skuas, auks, are in the Order *Charadriiformes* which is a large Order containing nearly 300 species. By the end of 1974 approximately 200 stamps illustrated clearly recognisable birds of this Order. There were besides many stamps showing "seagulls" which are unidentifiable and a decision whether to collect or ignore these will be necessary.

We can add to this nucleus collection some of the species in another six Orders. Those delightful characters, the penguins (*Sphenisciformes*) have 15 species and are so popular that some 40 stamps have been issued showing penguins swimming, waddling and resting, and some also depict large fluffy-coated youngsters. The pelicans, gannets, boobies, tropic-birds, frigate-birds, cormorants and darters are collected together into the Order *Pelecaniformes*, and this group has 110 stamps. The birds which inhabit the oceans successfully by flying above the waves for the greater

Sea-birds. Pitcairn 1964 4d White Tern; French Southern & Antarctic Terr. 1959 Light-mantled Sooty Albatross; Pitcairn 1964 2/6 White-chinned Petrel; Argentine 1961 Penguin & Chick; Dubai 1968 Lesser Black-backed Gull; Ifni 1952 Shag.

part of their lives, are in the Order *Procellariiformes*. The albatrosses, shearwaters and petrels belong to this Order, and the 30 stamps give a good overall picture of the birds flying, and at rest on oceanic islands and rocky shores where they nest.

Two further, very small, groups could be added at little extra cost. There are only four stamps showing divers (*Gaviiformes*) and 14 depicting grebes (*Podicipitiformes*) which are to be seen at sea as well as on inland waters.

This collection of sea-birds on stamps would be contained on 500 stamps. The collector might like to explore the possibility of adding some shore birds, such as the Rock Pipits which are rarely found far from the sea, and the sea-ducks. The subject can be interpreted in so many ways and could even be expanded to include all water birds if the collector so wished.

Books:

LOCKLEY, R. M. *Ocean wanderers: the migratory sea birds of the world.* 1974. David & Charles.

SPARKS, J. & SOPER, T. *Penguins.* 1967. David & Charles.

TUCK, G. S. *A Field-guide to the Seabirds of the world.* 1976. Collins.

Collecting Ducks, Geese and Swans on stamps

The waterfowl Order, *Anseriformes*, contains some 150 species, of which one third have appeared on 205 stamps. This group of attractive species might well appeal to wildfowlers as an interesting small stamp collection, having the advantage of being very well documented. It could, however, be an expensive collection, if it included a classic Black Swan.

Ducks, Geese and Swans. Poland 1970 Mallard; Roumania 1965 Mute Swan; Canada 1950 Canada Goose; Falkland Is. 1938 Upland Goose; Finland 1956 Whooper Swans.

A wildfowler might decide to omit the swans, as being protected from the gun by law, and select only the relevant ducks and geese from the family *Anatidae*. The keen sportsman might add to these some species from other Orders, e.g. grouse, ptarmigan, partridges and pheasant (*Galliformes*), plus waders, snipe and woodcock (from *Charadriiformes*) and add the Wood Pigeon. Should this collection still prove too small, the game birds of all countries could be studied and collected.

Books:
DELACOUR, J. *The Waterfowl of the world*. 4 vols. 1954–64. Country Life.
SCOTT, SIR P. *A Coloured key to the Wildfowl of the world*. 1969. H. F. & G. Witherby.

Collecting Game Birds on stamps
These birds are collected together in a complex Order called *Galliformes*, in which there are seven Families with some 250 species. The most popular Family is *Phasianidae*, including the quails, partridges and pheasants, of which the latter assume the larger number of both species and stamps. This

Game Birds. Poland 1970 Black Grouse; Bulgaria 1967 Pheasant; Cuba 1967 Golden Pheasant; San Marino 1960 Red-legged Partridge.

Family alone accounts for 125 of the 200 stamps which illustrate *Galliformes*. The beautiful colouring of the pheasants is an obvious attraction, though their long tails present difficulties to the designers. Sometimes a whole issue or set has been devoted to pheasants, e.g. Bhutan 1968.
The favourite subject in this group is the familiar Pheasant *Phasianus colchicus* with its subspecies. Nineteen countries have depicted it 21 times over. The Capercaillie, perhaps surprisingly, is a bird which has also attracted a good deal of attention from 13 European countries. It is a showy bird by habit though sombrely-clad like many of the rest of the Order, to which pheasants are an exception.

Books:
DELACOUR, J. & AMADON, D. *Curassows and related birds.* 1973. (New York).
DELACOUR, J. *The Pheasants of the world.* 1951.
WAYRE, P. *A Guide to the Pheasants of the world.* 1969. Country Life.

Collecting Pigeons and Doves on stamps
This is a large Order, *Columbiformes*, of some 300+ species, which has not been well illustrated on stamps. Just under 100 stamps depict pigeons and doves. No picture of an identifiable wild species was issued before 1948 and a complete collection, not too expensive, could be assembled with relative ease. Pigeons have a gentle charm and though some have beautiful colouring, their tones are usually muted. The pigeon-fancier would most probably make a sub-collection of the domestic and fancy pigeons shown on stamps, especially the birds illustrated from the recurring International Pigeon Exhibition which are featured by Hungary in some sets.
For any collector of this group of birds a very difficult decision would have to be made at an early stage. Will the very large number of "Peace Doves" and stylised doves be included or excluded? Apart from the 96 stamps clearly depicting different species of *Columbiformes* there is a similar number of Peace Doves—probably more. One has only to

glance at the section of the world catalogue of stamps dealing with the issues of the United Nations, to be speedily made aware that it is essential to decide whether to collect selectively, or to keep peace doves as a separate "species" on their own.

Collectors of pigeons and doves (and the Dodo!) are fortunate in having an authoritative and up to date monograph on their subject, written by a member of the staff of the British Museum (Natural History) and illustrated by Robert Gillmor.

Book:

GOODWIN, D. *Pigeons and Doves of the world*. 2nd ed 1970. British Museum (Nat. Hist.).

Pigeons and Doves. Germany DR 1968 Wood Pigeon; Mauritius 1965 12c Dodo (ext); Mauritius 1965 60c Dutch Pigeon (ext); Somaliland 1953 Somali Stock Dove.

Collecting Birds of Prey on stamps

This would form a very exciting and interesting collection with plenty of scope from the number of stamps available. The birds in the Order *Falconiformes* are popular with stamp-producers and some 300 stamps depict clearly illustrated eagles, hawks and falcons. Birds of prey are to be found all over the world, so that a large number of countries is involved, and with island forms in good supply a very detailed study of their classification and arrangement could be made. Added to this, there are some excellent modern monographs which would be a delight to own, and are very well illustrated.

To the stamps showing species of *Falconiformes* could be added those depicting owls. Only a very small number of stamps illustrates members of the owl Order *Strigiformes* and these, 32 stamps, when added to the *Falconiformes* would give a satisfactory "Birds of Prey" collection.

The only difficulties which one can foresee are the number of stylised eagles, eagles as part of coats of arms (which should be omitted), and the fact that eagles are usually regarded as being such aristocratic birds that they are used for the higher denominations on surface mail stamps and also appear regularly on "Air" stamps. Condors and vultures, especially such rare species as the Andean Condor, are

Birds of Prey. Mongolia 1970 Buzzard; Spanish Sahara 1974 Eared Vulture; Poland 1964 Osprey; Uruguay 1968 Great Horned Owl.

treated with similar respect and are expensive to purchase. Falconry has its devotees, and a small side-collection of falconry stamps could be brought together. The Arab countries (Abu Dhabi in particular) issue many birds of prey on stamps—some shown on a glove, with or without jesses. As may be expected, the Peregrine is the favourite falcon and appears in recognisable form on over 20 stamps. There are also many unidentifiable falcons and eagles for the curious to ponder.

Books:
BROWN, L. & AMADON, D. *Eagles, Hawks & Falcons.* 2 vols. 1969 (reprint Country Life 1975).
BURTON, J. A. *Owls of the World.* 1973. Peter Lane.
GROSSMAN, M. D. & HAMLET, J. *Birds of Prey of the world.* 1965. Cassell.
SPARKS, J. & SOPER, T. *Owls, their natural and unnatural history.* 1970. David & Charles.

Collecting Parrots on stamps
If you collect Parrots, you will have a most colourful assortment of stamps. It is an extremely attractive group, for not only are the birds bright and showy, but the stamps illustrating them are vivid little pictures, and to cap it all, there is a magnificent monograph, by J. M. Forshaw which you will have a good excuse to buy. This is costly but will be the standard book on the subject for the next 50 years at least, and can only increase in value as that time goes by. All the subspecies with their distribution are listed, and the plates are magnificent so that it is very easy to find out which species or subspecies has appeared on the stamps. In fact, this book will save the lazy stamp collector the work of doing his own research into the ornithological side of his subject. If you add to this basic volume a charming little book by Prestwich which tells how the birds got their names and who christened them, that side of things is complete.

Turning to the stamps themselves, we find that about 150 have been printed illustrating some 60 of the known 301 species of the Order *Psittaciformes.* Of these, the most frequently depicted are the African Grey Parrot, the Gold and Blue Macaw, and the Scarlet Macaw.

The parrot stamps cover the full range of prices to be paid for stamps. The early issues of the strange Kaka and Kea of New Zealand are very expensive, but many of the recent, well-printed stamps cost only a few pence.

Books:

FORSHAW, J. M. *Parrots of the world.* 1974. Lansdowne, Melbourne.

PRESTWICH, A. A. *A Guide to the names of parrots* (with their derivations). 1969.

Parrots. New Zealand 1965 Kaka; Malawi 1968 Lilian's Lovebird; Sp. Guinea 1957 African Grey Parrot; St. Lucia 1969 St. Lucia Amazon; Papua, New Guinea 1967 Vulturine Parrot.

Collecting Herons, Ibises, Spoonbills and Bitterns on stamps

These species are *Ciconiiformes* and among them the familiar Grey Heron and a British rarity, the Great White Heron or Egret, both being favourite birds with stamp designers. Over a dozen stamps illustrate the grey bird and nearly thirty the white one. The White Stork, however, eclipses them both, with 33 stamps devoted to it—not counting those curious all-white storks which carry babies (e.g. Iran 1970) in their oddly-coloured beaks. The birds are very stately and large, with long thin necks and legs which are not easy to compose in a good design on a small postage stamp. The way they have been accommodated by artists and designers shows much ingenuity on their part.

Heron, Ibis, Spoonbill. Fiji 1968 Reef Heron; Montserrat 1970 Little Blue Heron; Uganda 1965 Sacred Ibis; Senegal 1974 Spoonbills; Czech. 1960 Night Heron; Burundi 1965 African Jabiru.

There are about 125 stamps showing members of the *Ciconiiformes*, but there is no complete monograph on them and a good deal of ornithological research needs to be done by the collector of this group.

Book:

PETERS, J. L. *Checklist of the Birds of the World* Vol. 1. 1931.

Collecting Cranes, Rails and Bustards on stamps

The *Gruiformes* are divided into eleven Families, but representatives of only four of these Families have appeared on stamps. This shows a strange lack of interest in this attractive Order of birds which takes its name from the Latin word Grus, meaning a Crane, and the stamps showing birds of this Order depict 12 crane species—three of which are very popular. These are the European Crane *Grus grus* on 16 stamps; the Manchurian species *Grus japonensis* on 18 stamps; and the Crowned Crane *Balearica pavonina* on 29 stamps. The 17 species of rails (*Rallidae*) appear on 25 stamps, and the few Bustards (*Otidae*) on 27 stamps. The surprise in this group is found in the family *Rhinochetidae* especially formed for the strange Kagu. New Caledonia has used this unique bird on 42 of its stamps, whilst the islands of Wallis & Futuna, a dependency of New Caledonia added another 12 Kagus between 1920 and 1922. This group offers a philatelist a wide range of just under 200 stamps, old and new, to study.

Cranes, Rails, Kagus. Canada 1955 Whooping Crane; New Caledonia 1948 Kagu; Samoa 1967 Purple Swamp Hen; Pitcairn 1964 Henderson Is. Rail.

Books:
PETERS, J. L. *Checklist of the Birds of the world*. Vol. 2. 1934.

WALKINSHAW, L. H. *Cranes of the world*. 1974. Winchester.

Collecting Kingfishers, Bee-eaters, Rollers and Hoopoes on stamps

Seven Families of tropical and subtropical landbirds are grouped together in the Order *Coraciiformes*—most of them brightly coloured. They include the brilliant kingfishers (over 60 stamps), pretty todies and motmots, beautiful bee-eaters (40 stamps), cheerful rollers (36 stamps), the hoopoes (32 stamps of which 27 depict *Upupa epops*) and the peculiar hornbills which have such foul nesting habits (46 stamps)—in all nearly 250 stamps.

Kingfisher, Bee-eater, Roller, Hoopoe. Botswana 1967 Yellow-billed Hornbill; Rwanda 1967 Woodland Kingfisher; Bechuanaland 1961 African Hoopoe; El Salvador 1963 Turquoise-browed Motmot; Gambia 1966 Blue-bellied Roller; Ethiopia 1966 Blue-fronted Bee-eater.

Book:

PETERS, J. L. *Checklist of the Birds of the world*. Vol. 5. 1945.

Collecting Perching birds on stamps

If anyone contemplates collecting all the stamps depicting members of this very large Order, *Passeriformes*, it would be as well for him to know what he undertakes. There are some 880 stamps illustrating birds in this Order of approximately 5,110 species in about 57 Families (the scientists do not agree on the exact numbers). It is a wonderfully rich field for the enthusiast, but it would take a lot of organising and a detailed knowledge of the birds would be a decided asset before commencing work on such a large project.

The Order includes delicate little flycatchers and wrens of all hues (so unlike our British sombrely-clad Wren), brilliant pittas, charming titmice, and the exotic bower birds and birds of paradise. Also, there are birds with curious nesting habits like mudnest builders and those species which build such intricate nests that they are collectively known as weavers. It is an eye-opener to discover brilliantly-coloured jays and magpies, not to mention starlings, and the wealth of gaudy little birds which grace the album pages under scientific names for which there is no satisfactory English equivalent. A medium-sized album can successfully accommodate the stamps which make up the gallery of perching and song birds—and leafing through it gives one a wonderful impression of colour and variety of shape and form.

Books:

GRUSON, E. S. *A Checklist of the Birds of the world*. 1976. Collins.

PETERS, J. L. *Checklist of Birds of the world*. Vols 7–15. 1951–1970 (vols 8 & 11 not yet published).

Some small groups which are not feasible as separate collections

To make a worthwhile collection which is going to give pleasure and stimulate interest over a number of years, it is necessary for the number of stamps available to be at least a few hundred. So, we shall assume that fewer than a hundred stamps means the collection, except as a subsidiary interest, is not a worthwhile project. Below is a list of the other Orders of birds too small to collect as a main subject, though in the sections detailing possible collections in the foregoing pages I have indicated a few combinations which include some of these Orders.

Ostriches (*Struthioniformes*)	37 stamps
Rheas (*Rheiformes*)	4 stamps
Kiwis (*Apterygiformes*)	23 stamps
Cassowaries, Emus (*Casuariiformes*)	11 stamps
Tinamou (*Tinamiformes*)	1 stamp
Divers (*Gaviiformes*)	4 stamps
Grebes (*Podicipitiformes*)	14 stamps
Penguins (*Sphenisciformes*)	40 stamps
Tubenoses (*Procellariiformes*)	31 stamps
Flamingoes (*Phoenicopteriformes*)	46 stamps
Cuckoos (*Cuculiformes*)	39 stamps
Owls (*Strigiformes*)	32 stamps
Nightjars (*Caprimulgiformes*)	3 stamps
Trogons (*Trogoniformes*)	41 stamps
Swifts, Hummingbirds (*Apodiformes*)	29 stamps
Mousebirds (*Coliiformes*)	1 stamp
Woodpeckers, Toucans (*Piciformes*)	75 stamps

To collect all the non-passerine bird stamps would involve approx.	2,340 stamps
To collect all the passerine bird stamps would involve approx.	880 stamps
To collect all clearly identifiable birds would involve approx.	3,220 stamps

Other ornithological groupings
Other ornithological groupings would demand greater knowledge of birds than the suggestions made above. For those with such knowledge, I include the following schemes.

When authors first wrote about birds, they divided them into two basic categories: Land Birds and Water Birds, and it would be possible to adopt these to form collections. They would each form a large collection of stamps. We have already discussed the feasibility of building up a collection of stamps depicting sea-birds i.e. sea-going and sea-shore birds. To these could be added salt-marsh birds, birds of estuaries, sand dunes and shingles and sea cliffs. Freshwater birds would provide a much smaller collection of diverse species—dippers, wagtails, kingfishers, martins, sedge and reed birds, coots and moorhens, swans, some ducks, grebes and even fishing birds of prey like the Osprey and White-tailed Eagle. Whether or not the birds of water-side vegetation should be included, is a matter for individual preference. Land birds could be grouped by habitat—built-up areas with parks, gardens and orchards; farm-land; moors, heaths and downlands; inland cliffs, quarries and pits; uplands and mountains; woodland and forest; deserts.

Another possibility for largish collections would be based on "Zonation" (see A. L. Thomson p. 206). The birds of the tropics would form a most colourful group; another zone is the north temperate area, which, with the subarctic and arctic forms the northern hemisphere with its divers, grouse, auks and other familiar species. Proceeding southwards from the equator we have the south temperate zone which, coupled with the antarctic zone (and its sea-bird population) forms the southern hemisphere characterised by penguins, sheathbills, and the pelican Order.

No doubt other ideas will occur to the seasoned bird-watcher and keen ornithologist. Whatever the choice, however, a list of the species should be first drawn up, and checked against the list of species on stamps, to see if an interesting collection could be formed and studied.

Book:
THOMSON, A. L. *editor. A New Dictionary of birds.* 1964. Nelson.

Tropical birds.

6

One Thousand and One Decisions

Well over 3,000 stamps with an identifiable bird species forming part of the motif have been issued. There are, besides, over 1,000 stamps which depict birds, not always recognisable, some very small, or only occupying one quarter of the stamp. All bird stamp collectors will have to make the decision whether to include or exclude them. As the decision is inevitable, it is better made at the beginning, rather than at a later stage of collecting, so as to save valuable resources—time, money and stationery. Having decided which categories to include in your collection it is helpful to make a list of "Policy Decisions".

We shall deal with the categories likely to be problematical under two headings:

(a) Bird stamps likely to be excluded from any collection

(b) Bird stamps which might be included or excluded

(a) Bird stamps likely to be excluded from any collection
Stamps whose **physical shape** is that of a bird—Sierra Leone specialises in issuing oddly-shaped stamps, some in the shape of the map of the country Sierra Leone, others oval, or trefoil, and in 1969 a set of 6 eagle-shaped stamps embossed on black paper (repeated in 1970 on white paper). The eagle is stylised and unidentifiable, and though a delightfully eccentric set of stamps, it does not really qualify for a place in a bird stamp collection.

Just as artists frequently place a small "V" in the sky in their paintings, with no particular species in mind and no thought of the viewer trying to discover which species was intended, so some designers of stamps include these symbolic signs to represent birds on stamps. Since they are too small to be identified, such items should be ignored.

This brings us to the question of other stylised or **symbolic birds**. A large number of stamps depict this type of bird. Apart from the hundreds of "Peace Doves" which immediately spring to mind, there are "pigeon post" pigeons and messengers carrying letters in their beaks, eagles as symbols of strength, the "Golden bird of Japan", and the Gallic Cock, all of which are troublesome birds since they are recognisable as coming from a certain bird Order, or Family, but are not true wild species. A whole collection could be devoted to Peace Doves because they are so numerous, but apart from many issued by the United Nations, the curious fact about these doves, is that they usually come from countries in the communist bloc which are armed to the teeth. Owls, as symbols of wisdom sometimes appear, e.g. Great Britain 1961 3d (a tiny bird, upper right, symbolic of the wisdom of saving), and Belgium 1946 (65c + 75c).

Stylised birds prove very much more difficult. Many of the earliest stamps used stylised birds taken from their national coats of arms, or used their "national" bird and stylised it for repeated use over many years, e.g. the stylised Bald Eagle of the U. S. A. 1869, 1875 and 1903. If it is obvious they are stylised *Bald* Eagles there might be a case for including them, since they are an identifiable species, but in a large collection of bird stamps with plenty of naturally-drawn examples of the same species, the stylised forms should be excluded.

W. F. Stanley, in *Birds of the World on Stamps*, is careful to note stylised forms and these can easily be picked out from his lists when making the decision whether to include them or not. Note his opinion on the stylising of a Swallow (S. Korea 1960); an Ostrich (Somalia 1965); the Emus of Australia's stamps 1913, 1914–30, 1931–6, 1949–50; the Netherlands Swan of 1943 and Peru's 1960 Cormorant.

Another point to note here, is that the White Storks which

appear carrying babies invariably have all-white plumage and are therefore symbolic only, and not the true species of White Stork which has at least half of each wing feather distinctly black in colour. Iran 1970 8r is an example of the symbolic white stork.

Coats of arms sometimes incorporate birds in their designs. The stamps using coats of arms, however, are designed to depict the whole coat of arms, not individual parts of it, and the birds are only a fractional proportion of the design and too small to be admitted as bird stamps. Beware of the Brown Pelicans and Flamingoes in Turks and Caicos arms (1966, 1967, 1970) and other species in Mexico's stamps of 1900–61, Antigua 1951, Barbados 1931 and a host of others.

Legendary and mythical birds should also be excluded—on the grounds that they are birds of the imagination, rather than scientific reality. Occasionally Aesop's *Fables* are depicted, and scenes from nursery stories e.g. 1972 Niger Republic included fables of the fox and crow in their set, and Hans Andersen's ugly duckling was figured in 1935 by Denmark. The impish Nils Holgersson riding on the back of a snow white goose, derived from Selma Lagerloff's "The Wonderful Adventures of Nils" (Sweden 1971) is charming, but if one buys such material, where will it end?

Phoenixes there are in plenty, and we know their legend, but what of the Kalavinka of Japan (1961 and 1966) and the Turul of Hungary (between 1900 and 1916 there were over 100 Turuls on stamps). Five stamps referring to Cambodian legends were issued in 1957. This material is interesting, but hardly relevant to a serious bird stamp collection.

The Gallic Cock of France; Character from Swedish story about Nils, and the white snow goose; The mythical Turul of the Magyars.

Artistic birds. Many bird paintings have been reproduced on stamps. We must distinguish carefully between bird paintings executed as scientifically accurate portraits of the birds for identification purposes by artists specialising in bird paintings or natural history painters, and paintings by famous artists which included birds. The latter frequently painted fanciful birds for which no live counterparts can be found. The bird-artists' work is discussed in Chapter 8, so we need deal only with other types of bird paintings here.

In the past few years a number of sets have appeared reproducing famous paintings which included birds, some of them accurate species and others (sometimes in the same set) unidentifiable species e.g. China (Formosa) 1969 where 3 stamps have clear pictures and a fourth ($5) an unidentifiable bird. Two western-style bird paintings reproduced on stamps were issued by Roumania in 1970 as part of a set of sporting pictures in Roumanian galleries. They depicted a spaniel and pheasant (by deduction *Phasianus colchicus*) by J. B. Oudry and a game dealer's stall by F. Snyder.

Apart from paintings, more birds taken from other art forms, have been featured on stamps. One or two sets include bird mosaics, from mosaic tiled floors and walls. An example of this kind of bird mosaic on stamps may be seen on the 1972 Dahomey set of air "Save Venice" stamps, reproduced from mosaics in St Mark's Basilica.

Birds in pottery i.e. tureen birds and jugs, have also appeared on stamps e.g. San Marino's "Duck Jug" of 1971 in a set showing examples of Etruscan art. A pheasant incense burner after Ninsei was used for the design of the 50y value of Japan 1969.

There are many others, but our concern is with true species of wild birds, so we shall not linger any longer among these artistic species which have no place in our album of true bird species.

(b) Bird stamps which might be included or excluded
Some of the decisions in this group are difficult to make. Apart from the merits and demerits of the stamps, a major factor in deciding whether or not to collect them will be the

nature and size of your main collection. If you already have a large number of good bird stamps to purchase, then this fringe material might well be excluded on the grounds of cost or as an aid to reduce the size of the collection. If your main collection is a small one, and you find some of this type of material particularly interesting, then there is no reason why you should not include it.

There are some very attractive sets of stamps depicting either **Domestic or semi-domestic** birds. Domestic hens, geese, pigeons and ducks have all appeared on stamps. I counted 70 such stamps up to the end of 1969, but lost track of them after that—there are so many. The subject is thus large enough to make a subsidiary collection.

Hungary was the venue of the International Pigeon Fancier's Exhibition in 1957–8 and again in 1969, and fancy pigeon stamps were issued to commemorate the event. More strange-looking pigeons turned up on the North Viet-Nam issue of 1968, and in 1964 North Korea illustrated some barnyard fowl of quite surprising charm. Canary breeding was featured on some Cuban stamps in 1969 but otherwise cage birds do not appear to have much popularity. There are so many beautiful wild species illustrated on stamps that it is better to collect them than these captives, cooped up in cages and bred to produce distortions and absurdities.

Heads only—Occasionally the artist has chosen to draw only the head of a bird, utilising to the best advantage the small space on the face of a stamp. It makes for variety in the

Heads only. French Guinea 1962 African Grey Parrot; Fernando Poo 1964 Great Blue Touraco; Nauru 1966 White Tern.

album, but is not an example one would like to see emulated too frequently. The latest example is the Papua & New Guinea set of 3 issued in 1974, an earlier set being Guinea 1962, and an ostrich head from Spanish Sahara in 1952. Another four heads, of a Greylag Goose, Lapwing, White Stork and Kestrel were drawn at the Zwin Nature Reserve for a set of Belgian stamps in 1972.

Composite pictures with many motifs in the design may have two or more birds, or a bird and another non-ornithological motif. Where a stamp is designed in two halves, one half being devoted to a picture of a bird, and that clearly identifiable, there is really no reason (unless one has an otherwise very large collection) why such a stamp should not be included. However, if the bird is one of several motifs, and very small, it should be omitted e.g. the tiny Quetzal on the "Visit Guatemala" propaganda stamp of 1968 which had four other small scenes in the same design.

Flocks of Birds. Canada Geese 1963; Umm-al-Qiwain 1972 Emperor Penguins; St Pierre & Miquelon 1973 Puffins; Senegal 1974 Flamingoes (se-tenant).

A number of birds on one stamp present equal difficulties. When there are two birds illustrated, one always hopes the two belong to the same Genus or Family, then placing them in a scientifically classified album and cataloguing and listing them will require fewer cross references. Otherwise, it may be simpler to purchase two copies of the stamp. Should there be more than two species, the pictures are likely to be too small to be worth adding to the collection. However, if a flock of birds of the same species is shown on one stamp, then the decisions are first, is the species identifiable, second is it a quality stamp (in design, colour, accurate drawing).

Where one design is repeated in later issues, with changes of currency, alteration of colour, or overprinted with some lettering, the question arises whether to collect all **Varieties**, or just the original issue. Philatelists find these variations fascinating, and would wish to collect them all and carefully catalogue them. So would anyone with a small group of stamps to collect who is also interested in postal history. If you are interested solely, or mainly, in the birds depicted, you will want the clearest pictures of the birds and might well select only those issued with no words obliterating part of the portrait of the bird. This will take careful thought and investigation before each case is decided on its own merits. Buying all varieties bulks out a collection and adds to the expense—but also adds greatly to the interest.

Local issues are another special case. These stamps are used for payment within a restricted area, sometimes issued by a town council, an island and even by a commercial organisation. The majority of local posts have already been thoroughly investigated by researchers, and catalogued by study circles, and there have been several world lists published. Even so, though well-known and documented, locals are scarce material and not easy to collect. The bird stamps issued by local authorities are included by W. F. Stanley and number just under 90 stamps of colourful attractive design. One third of this number depict sea-birds—as might be expected since most of the local issues are from island postal authorities. This might influence a collector of "Sea-birds on Stamps" to include locals, but deter other collectors.

UFOs galore—On stamps there are far too many unidentified flying objects, which present something of a problem to a bird stamp collector. Stanley lists at least 200, not counting long runs of sets and repetitions of the same design over a number of years. Some of the stamps with an unidentifiable species occur in a set which otherwise illustrates clearly recognisable species. In this case, even if you do not want to collect UFOs you will acquire some! They are best mounted on a page at the back of the album and a spare idle hour may be spent occasionally trying to identify them, or they can be quietly forgotten. Alternatively, unidentified birds could be grouped together in Family or Order sections at the end of the appropriate group in the album e.g. West Irian's 1968 75s is obviously a Cassowary—but which one? Put it on an album leaf by itself at the end of the section of Cassowaries. Similarly with the many penguins, albatrosses, pelicans, herons, swans and geese, vultures, eagles and falcons, cranes, gulls and terns, parrots, hornbills, toucans, etc.

UFOs are better not purchased (except where this is unavoidable when one occurs in the middle of a good set), or their purchase postponed until all the very good bird stamps within your subject have been bought, catalogued, mounted and studied.

Appendix items. The items in the Appendix to Gibbons' *Stamps of the World* catalogue represent another special category on which we must make up our minds whether to include or exclude them. The main difficulty here is that countries whose stamps are listed in the Appendix because they "persist in issuing far more stamps than can be justified by postal needs . . ." may at some future date be returned to the main body of the catalogue. Indeed, this has already happened. The following countries (which issued bird stamps) were in the 1975 Appendix but restored to the main body of the 1976 catalogue: Burundi 1968-, Dubai 1968-, Panama 1965-9, Qatar 1966-. Had a collector refrained from buying these stamps in 1975 he might regret that decision in 1976. In the 1976 Appendix nearly 200 bird stamps were listed, and this is quite a large number to consider. The greater proportion of these had been issued by Middle East countries, and anyone collecting Palaearctic species would find many items in the Appendix—not fully listed, but with such sparse information as:

"SHARJAH 1972 Birds 1st series, 20, 25, 75d, Air 1, 2r"

W. F. Stanley, working from the American Scott *Stamp Catalogue* and the Minkus Catalogue, lists them in full. To add to the difficulties, some of these Arab issues are of doubtful authenticity, sets having been placed on the market after the state had joined the United Arab Emirates in 1972 and no longer issued their own stamps e.g. Sharjah 1972 issues. The firm of Gibbons does not sell these stamps and they are not easily found except in incomplete, cancelled to order sets done up in packets and sold by newsagents and sweet shops. The Appendix items form the most formidable problem to be resolved by any collector.

Other kinds of stamps and "postal stationery" (for want of a better phrase) are frequently ignored by the serious collector, but might appeal to anyone with a small bird stamp collection who would like to have all kinds of stamps illustrating his special bird species. This kind of material is cheap, largely because serious philatelists do not collect it. A few miniature sheets include bird portraits, but these are rarely used and not all of them are placed on sale in post offices. Coil stamps (used in stamp machines) are listed in Gibbons and some recent examples are Birds of Paradise (stylised) from Papua and New Guinea 1969 2c and 5c. Express letter stamps, postage due, charity and official stamps all occasionally have birds as their main design e.g. Bahawalpur's Pelicans of 1945 on official stamps, the express letter stamps of Andorra 1928 ("Eagle" over Pyrenees) and Mauritania's 16 attractive postage due stamps of 1963. Postal labels are issued for airmail, registration and similar purposes, and are part of the postal system history of a country. Sometimes changes of government policy mean that postage stamps are authorised for fiscal use, with no change in design but overprinted ". . . & Revenue" to indicate their fiscal use. Some very attractive British stamp booklets have had covers printed with pictures of birds, and there are other examples from foreign countries. Telegraph stamps (intended for payment of telegraph communications) could also be searched for bird designs. This material is all very fascinating and may supplement and add to the interest of the stamps themselves.

Postage Due.—3 of set of Mauritania 1963.

These are the main queries and problems which I have had to solve whilst collecting bird stamps, and no doubt there will be others which will occur, especially for anyone collecting selectively.

7

A Chapter of Errors

When selecting an article for purchase, most people carefully inspect each item and reject imperfect examples, or, if they are prepared to accept a small fault, request a reduction in the price. The philatelist is a strange exception to this general rule. In fact, some philatelists become quite obsessed in their search for imperfection. They prize a stamp showing a bird deprived of its legs or with a wrongly coloured eye, more highly than a stamp depicting a bird in perfect health and plumage, and are willing to pay more for it. Error-spotting is part of the philately game, and, should you be so fortunate as to find a colour is missing from the printing on one of your stamps, or you own a one-legged bird, you might even be led to think that collecting bird stamps is financially rewarding—provided you are willing to sell. Gibbons' stamp catalogues show some of the errors in their illustrations and note others in their lists, along with the price paid for these expensive mistakes.

A famous printing error is the Quetzal of Guatemala ,which on the 2c green and brown stamp of 1881 was accidentally printed upside down. In 1968 Nigeria celebrated the 5th anniversary of the Federal Republic with a 1/6d stamp depicting a dove. A variety of this stamp shows Nigeria's dove with a green feather in its usually all-white tail The printers of the Mauritius stamps of 16 March 1965 had a disastrous series of faulty printing of colours resulting in broken claws and missing legs. British Honduras managed to give its jacana white (or unprinted) legs on the 3c value of 1962, and this is to name but a few of the many printing errors.

Millie the Billingual Parrot.
Guyana 1967 Blue & Gold Macaw.

Incorrect naming of bird species in the catalogue is not always the fault of the cataloguer, for he is sometimes misled by wrong names on the stamps themselves. Guyana issued a set of two stamps at Christmas 1967 and repeated the issue, with different coloured backgrounds in January 1968. The same bird appeared on all the stamps, with her name also inscribed—"Millie the Bilingual Parrot". Millie, however, was undisputedly a Blue and Gold Macaw (*Ara ararauna*). She was quite a character, and when taken to the Montreal Expo Exhibition of 1967, she disgraced herself by swearing profusely in English and French! Have a look at Togo's set of exotic birds in 1972, with four whydahs and one parakeet. The parakeet is surely wrongly labelled on the stamp. It is much more like *Psittacula krameri* with its green head, and not *P. cyanocephala* as on the stamp. The editor of Gibbons' *Stamps of the World* catalogue spotted this one, and noted it as being the Ring-necked Parakeet *P. krameri*. Where two species are similar in plumage, though widely separated in distribution, some amusing mistakes occur. Guyana has nominated the orange feathered Cock-of-the-Rock as its national bird—and then pictured a red-plumaged species on its 1968 and 1969 stamps of 25c value. The drawing is correct, with the carefully marked crest feathers of the orange bird clearly shown, but the colouring has gone wrong. The red coloured Cock-of-the-Rock is not found in Guyana, but in the northern Andes from Colombia to Peru.

I have found some faulty spelling on a few stamps, and expect you will soon find some more. Argentine Republic, 1974 Children's Welfare 70c + 30c depicts *Sphorophila caerulescens*, but the printer has given it the name *S. caeru-*

lescems. Albania's bird set of 15th November 1968 included a 50q Long-tailed Tit *Aegithalos caudatus* which became *Aegithalus caodatus.* Ajman bee-eaters seem not to eat bees, but become Bea-eaters instead (1971 3d Red-bearded Bea-eater). The reasons for faulty spelling may be just careless copying of the scientific name, but getting the wrong scientific name altogether is not always the fault of the artist and designer. If they use a bird book published some years previously, the names might well be out of date. Scientists are continually re-appraising birds' status in relation one to another, and will alter their names and positions in Families, etc. according to new discoveries.

Faulty Scientific Names on Stamps. Angola 1951 Bataleur Eagle Terathopius ecaudatus *Not Theratopius e.; Bhutan 1968 Sclater's Impeyan Pheasant, thus* Lophophorus sclateri *Not L. sclareti; Panama 1967 Belted Kingfisher* Ceryle alcyon *Not* Achloceoite amazona *which is Amazon Kingfisher. (Figure taken from Singer's book* Birds of the World *where it is correctly named).*

One of the most curious errors in bird stamps occurs in a Panama issue which is a most attractive set apart from one stamp. The 5c of 1967 is a macaw of some kind, but the colouring of its feathers bears no resemblance to any known species. The remaining five stamps in this set, however, are good reproductions of five illustrations by Arthur Singer in O. L. Austin's book *Birds of the World* (Hamlyn 1961). What went wrong?

Discovering what went wrong, and why, is all part of the enjoyment of bird-spotting on stamps.

8

Bird Stamp Artists and Designers

When a postal authority takes the decision to create an issue of stamps illustrating birds, the question as to which species are to be shown is the first consideration. Will it be a rare birds set, or a set with well-loved local species, or the most colourful birds, or game birds, and so on. Most authorities have hundreds of species in their own avifauna from which to choose a mere handful, for only rarely does a set include more than a dozen values. Hardly ever can we find out the reasons for their choice. Occasionally a modern designer will contribute an article to a stamp journal, or another author when writing about a new issue will interview the designer, and reveal how a set came into being. When there is a well-illustrated book about the birds of the region, a selection of these pictures may be used and copied for the stamps. Where this method has been adopted, we have some extremely well-designed and accurately portrayed birds forming a set of stamps. On the whole, one could say that using well-drawn book illustrations by eminent bird artists has produced the most beautiful bird stamps. But, during the last ten years or so we have had a series of such excellent sets designed by modern artists that they compare very favourably with the work of older bird artists.

Illustrations in books used as the basis for stamp designs
Quite a few sets are based on illustrations in bird books, and among them are some of the best drawn and designed stamps available to the bird stamp collector. In fact, if you wish to concentrate on collecting quality stamps selected for the accuracy of their portrayal of the species, these are the sets to

buy. I shall give details of some of the more obvious ones and you will find others which I have not space to mention.

Ramon de la Sagra (1801–1871) was director of the botanical gardens at Havana in 1822 and wrote a *Natural History of Cuba* between the years 1837 and 1839. On the centenary of his death, 10th December 1971, Cuba issued a set of 8 bird stamps based on the designs in his book.

Dr Claude Gay (1800–1873) was a French botanist who spent the years 1824–41 in Chile. He published a book on Chilean flora and fauna in 1848, and from this some illustrations were chosen—25 different botanical and zoological designs—which were each repeated three times in the denominations 60c, 2p60, and 3p, of Chile's *Centenary of Claude Gay's Book on Chilean Flora and Fauna* in 1948. The birds chosen were the Chilean Pigeon *Columba aracauna*, some tiny penguins (unidentifiable), Emperor Penguin *Aptenodytes forsteri*, the Crested Caracara *Polyborus plancus*, Red-gartered Coot *Fulica armillata* and the Chilean Torrent Duck *Merganetta armata*.

Two more South American countries took advantage of some very good illustrations, this time in a modern bird book. The author was O. L. Austin, and the artist Arthur Singer, for the book about *Birds of the World* (Hamlyn 1961) which gave a short account of each bird Family and illustrated typical forms for each. Panama was the first, with 7 birds in 1967. Unfortunately one value, the 5c, has somehow gone sadly awry and though it looks like a macaw, no known macaw has plumage of that colouring. Also, in the book the Double-collared Aracari is facing towards the right, but on the stamp it is reversed. Paraguay chose 9 quite different species from the same book, and in 1969 issued a bird set. The stamps are most attractive and their designer, C. Alonso, chose his subjects well, for these are some of Singer's most attractive illustrations.

The famous North American artist and author John James Audubon (1785–1851) produced extremely large plates of birds in his *Birds of America*, published in Britain between 1827 and 1838. Appropriately, the U.S.A. has used one of his paintings for two of their stamps. His Columbia Jays, or

Collie's Magpie Jays *Calocitta colliei* were chosen for the Audubon commemorative 5c stamp of 1963, and repeated on the 20c Air stamp of 1967. The two blue magpie-jays have been reproduced in their tiny format very well, considering they were reduced from a plate measuring $25\frac{3}{4}''$ × 38". In 1975 Haiti produced a long set of 23 stamps all based on Audubon's plates, but with unequal success. Audubon's very elaborate plates with scenic backgrounds and masses of foliage do not lend themselves to postage stamp size reproduction and some of the Haiti stamps are disastrously overcrowded. Where Audubon's simpler designs have been copied, the stamp is more successful. The designer of the Virgin Islands' stamps of 1956 recognised the fact that plain backgrounds are best for bird stamps, and when he copied Audubon's plate of the Brown Pelican ($2.40) he omitted the foliage. Audubon's plate of the Man-o'-war Bird *Fregata magnificens* had no background and was reproduced on the $4.80 stamp exactly as Audubon had designed his plate for *Birds of America.*

Dr Austin Roberts (1883–1948) published a book on *The Birds of South Africa* in 1940 whilst he was Curator of the Transvaal Museum and Zoological Gardens at Pretoria. This book was substantially revised in 1970 by Dr G. R. MacLachan and R. Liversidge. Malawi's new definitive issue of bird stamps, 13 values in 1975, were chosen partly from Roberts' revised book and partly from P. A. Clancey's *Game Birds of South Africa* published in 1971. Mr Clancey (1917–) was appointed Director of Durban Museum, Natal, in 1952. The stamps form one of the most delightful sets of recent years.

The British author, John Gould, issued 41 folio volumes with some 3,000 plates of birds, during his lifetime (1804–1881). His *Birds of Asia*, published in 7 volumes between 1850 and 1883 with 530 hand-coloured plates was used by Ajman to choose some illustrations for a set of 16 stamps issued as a two-part series of 8 stamps each in 1971. They make very pretty stamps, but the figures of the birds are too small to be successful.

Another very beautiful book, this time about Australasian

birds, was published in Britain in 1928, with a supplement in 1936. The hand-coloured lithographic plates of Gregory M. Mathews' *The Birds of Norfolk and Lord Howe Islands* were used for a remarkably restrained and aesthetically outstanding set of stamps issued by Norfolk Island in 1970–71. The 15 values formed their definitive set, which will surely be regarded as a ''classic'' set at some future date.

Norfolk Island—part of 1970 set of 15 values, designs from Matthews' book on Norfolk Island birds, illus. by a number of artists; 2c Norfolk Is. Thick head (Golden Whistler) drawn by H. Grönvold; 3c Norfolk Is. Flyeater, drawn by H. Grönvold; 9c Grey-headed Blackbird (Island Thrush), drawn by Roland Green; 30c Norfolk Island Fantail (Grey or White-shafted Fantail), drawn by H. Grönvold; 45c Norfolk Island Starling, drawn by H. Grönvold.

One of the artists for Mathews' book was Roland Green (1895–1972), and he designed the plate of the Grey-headed Blackbird illustrated in the figure above. He also had the doubtful distinction of having some of his illustrations in Pycraft's *Birds in Flight* (published in 1922) copied for a bogus issue of stamps issued in 1953 by Croatia—a postal authority which ceased issuing stamps in 1945! This very fine artist deserved a better fate than to have his excellent drawings used in this manner.

Another recent set of stamps whose designs reproduced

illustrations in a British bird book was issued by Oman in 1972. If these stamps are compared with the illustrations drawn by Benjamin Fawcett, the printer for F. O. Morris's *A History of British Birds*, published 1851–7 in 6 volumes with 357 hand-coloured wood-engravings, they will be seen to be based on his designs.

Some photographic book illustrations are now being used as the basis of stamp designs, for example, the photographs in E. T. Gilliard's *Living Birds of the World* (Hamilton 1958) have been used by some designers. Checking book illustrations against stamps would prove a rewarding study and it would be interesting to know the extent to which motifs have been copied from pictures of birds in books.

Some modern artists and designers

A number of excellent artists have been at work in recent years. Four outstanding artists whose work is to be seen on stamps are D. M. Reid-Henry, Don R. Eckelberry, Dick Findlay and Robert Gillmor. Mr Eckelberry specialises in painting North and Central American birds, and has also illustrated *Birds of the West Indies* by James Bond (it was from this book that Ian Fleming, who lived in Jamaica and was interested in its birds, took the author's name for his hero!) D. R. Eckelberry's designs appear on one West Indies stamp—the 10c of Trinidad and Tobago 1969, and on the very fine set of British Honduras 1962. This set of 12 stamps shows the birds perched on branches with little other detail to detract from the beautifully-drawn figures of the birds themselves.

David Reid-Henry was the son of another excellent artist George Henry, and was born in Ceylon. He was educated in England and enjoyed the friendship of the great bird painter George Lodge, whose tradition he inherited and so successfully keeps alive in his own distinctive style. His designs for Botswana 1967 and Mauritius 1965 and 1967 show clean, uncluttered profiles of the birds, on which great care was bestowed to produce perfect plumage details.

Dick Findlay's drawings of the "rare" (some are quite common) birds of South West Africa (1974 and 1975) are a

*Mauritius—part of the 1965 set of 15 values and 1967
Self Govt. set of 4 values, designed by D. M. Reid-
Henry; 2c 1965 Mauritius Grey White-eye; 10c 1967
Rodrigues Brush-Warbler; 3c 1965 Rodrigues Fody;
60c 1967 Rodrigues Parakeet; 4c 1965 Mauritius Olive
White-eye; 10c 1965 Mauritius Fody.*

*South West Africa—4 Rare Birds of S.W.A., drawn by
Dick Findlay, 1974. 4c White-tailed Shrike-Fly-
catchers; 5c Rosy-faced Lovebirds; 10c Damara Rock
Jumper; 15c Rüppell's Parrots.*

delight, and although there are background scenes and details (which usually clutter rather than enhance the design) somehow he gets away with it. We hope to see more of his work on stamps in the future.

Robert Gillmor's cards and other work for the Royal Society for the Protection of Birds have made his paintings deservedly popular and appreciated. He designed the most attractive set of stamps showing 6 of the rarest Seychelles birds in 1972, which were well reproduced lithographically.

Rare Seychelles Birds 1972 Designed by R. Gillmor. 5c Seychelles Brush Warbler; 20c Scops Owl; 50c Blue Pigeon; 65c Magpie Robin; 95c Black Paradise Fly-catcher; 3r50c Seychelles Kestrel.

Three lady artists deserve a note of praise for their very good designs. Mrs H. Temple-Watts' designs for Australia 1964–5 and 1966 are a diverse set, some of the stamps being rather more successful than others. Mrs C. Hughes produced three designs for Swaziland in 1962, 5c, 10c and 50c, of which the 10c Secretary Bird is very fine. Mrs Réna M. Fennessy is well known in East Africa for her bird paintings and she did the drawings for the 1965 Uganda long set of 14 values. This set has different-sized and shaped stamps, and Mrs Fennessy has shown great ingenuity in the choice and positioning of the birds in their frames. The foliage is printed very lightly in a pale shade or tint—again an imaginative method by which such detail is kept unobtrusive yet contributes another dimension to the design. Messrs Harrison are to be congratulated on their handling of the printing of this issue.

We cannot go on indefinitely naming all the good designers and artists, space will not allow, but a quick survey of some of the best sets and artists and designers working at the moment will be sufficient to draw attention to sets which are most worthy of purchase for their quality of design. If you buy stamps for these qualities, you should never overlook sets by V. Whiteley (Gambia 1966, Montserrat 1970, St Helena 1961, St Lucia 1969); G. Drummond (Bahamas 1974, British Solomon Islands 1975, Fiji 1971); R. Granger Barrett (British Indian Ocean Territory 1975, Lesotho 1971); Gandon, designer and engraver, (France 1957, 1960, French Guinea 1947, Mali 1965, Monaco 1955); M. Goaman (Cayman Is. 1974, Ghana 1959, Kenya 1964, Qatar 1961, St Vincent 1965, Fiji 1962-6, and see article on his work in *Stamp Monthly* Feb. 1974); and P. Lambert (New Caledonia 1970, Tchad 1961-3, St Pierre & Miquelon 1963, Upper Volta 1965). Other sets which should not be overlooked are Ascension 1963 (N. P. Ashmole) and both Cocos 1969 and Bechuanaland 1961 (P. Jones); the beautiful British Solomon Is. 1965 and Pitcairn Is. 1964 (M. C. Farrer Bell). San Marino, Yugoslavia and Switzerland have recently produced some of the best European bird designs, whilst Poland's "Game Birds" of 1970 and Hungary's bird set of 1973 designed by M. Füle are both very fine sets with sensitive colouring and drawing.

One should not neglect the sets designed corporately by studios—such as Waddington's of the U.S.A. and Ars Polona in Poland.

Monochrome bird stamps

These might not be to everyone's taste, but the fine line drawings give an aesthetically pleasing stamp if rather a severe design. There is an elegant beauty about the monochrome engraved stamp which is lacking in the highly-coloured designs of some of the lithographed stamps. Many of the Scandinavian stamps are produced in monochrome, and the Swedish stamps of 1958 with 5 of Bruno Liljefors' paintings (2 of them birds) have a very distinctive quality and appeal. Liljefors specialised in painting sea-birds, and the 30ö value shows a Great Black-backed Gull whilst the other 30ö stamp depicts a Golden Eagle and Crows. (*See* RUSSOW, K. E. *Bruno Liljefors: an appreciation*, pubd 1929 and Liljefors' own book *Ute I Markerna* with 33 col. pl. from his original paintings 2nd ed 1922). In the same tradition is the 1975 stamp, especially engraved on steel by Major Franzan-Matthews portraying a "cock of the woods" or Capercaillie. Other Scandinavian stamps in monochrome are the Danish designs of 1956, used also by Finland, Iceland and Sweden. The beautiful flying swans, *Cygnus cygnus* on all these stamps, were drawn by Viggo Bang, then engraved by Sven Ewert and printed in one colour, blue or rose. Still in the north, the Icelandic black and white Eiders with tinted background (a shoreline) and Icelandic Falcons of 1959 are well-designed stamps. Canada shows its "national" goose in monochrome on a number of finely-drawn stamps and the Great Northern Diver on another single issue to commemorate National Wildlife Week in 1957.

The German stamps, with the bird figure outline in black, printed on tinted paper, are models of refined good taste, particularly the small-sized stamps of Germany DR 1959. The Australian Lyrebirds and Kookaburras are further good examples of attractive stamps printed in one colour only. The Falkland Island stamps of· 1960 show a variation in that the birds are printed in black in one part of the stamp, and the small portion of the stamp with the Queen's head is tinted in delicate and delightful shades. The rather similar 1956 issue was printed entirely in one tint, both the bird and the rest of the stamp.

Monochrome Bird Stamps. Norfolk Is. 1961 Providence Petrel—printed in brown; Germany DR 1965 Goshawk— printed in black on red ground; Canada 1957 Great Northern Diver—printed in black; New Zealand 1958 Australian Gannet—printed in blue—entire stamp; Iceland 1959 Eider—printed in black, tinted green shore line; Falkland Is. 1960 Kelp Geese—printed in black, rest of stamp tinted rose; Sweden 1966 Great Black-backed Gull— printed in black; Christmas Is. 1963 Christmas Is. Frigate Bird—printed in green.

Distinctive Oriental Stamps

The stamps of China, Japan and Viet-Nam show the distinctive oriental style of painting, and some sets include bird paintings by old masters. One of the most popular stamps from this part of the world, is Hiroshige's Moon and (Bean) Geese (1949 Japan 8y) and it is quite expensive to buy in consequence. The Chinese cranes from paintings by Chen Chi-fo on the 3 values of 1962 are excellent examples of Chinese bird art.

Oriental Style Stamps. China (People's Rep.) 1962 Manchurian Cranes; Japan 1963/4 10y Bush Warbler; Japan 1975 20y Manchurian Crane; Viet-Nam North 1973 Grass Warblers.

The printers

Any design can be ruined by careless plate-preparation and printing. Some of the British printers excel in their sensitive and sympathetic cooperation with the artists and designers, and are responsible for many of the top quality sets of bird stamps. Messrs Harrison, using photogravure, have done a large number of clean-cut bird portraits with uncluttered backgrounds—the hall-mark of the best of the bird stamps. They have a fine collection to their credit, including Mauritius 1965, British Honduras 1962, Montserrat 1970, Bechuanaland 1961 and Botswana 1967, and The Gambia 1966 to name but a few. The studio of John Waddington Ltd (U.S.A.) has also produced some very good stamps, though some of the background tints are a little too deep and their pictures include more background detail e.g. St Vincent 1970. The Waterlow stamps, many in monochrome, are fine examples of expert printing.

The stamps mentioned above are a personal choice, of necessity, but I hope that by choosing some which I think good in both colour and design, and by figuring examples of quality stamps, I have drawn attention to yet another absorbing aspect of bird stamp collecting.

British Indian Ocean Territory, 11 of set of 15, issued Feb. 1975. Designed by Richard Granger Barrett. Drawn from birds common to the Territory. 5c Aldabra Drongo; 10c Malagasy Coucal; 20c Red-headed Forest Fody; 25c Fairy Tern; 30c Crested Tern; 40c Brown Booby; 50c Noddy; 60c Grey Heron; 65c Blue-faced Booby; 95c Malagasy White-eye; 1R Green-backed Heron.

9

A Guide to the Published Catalogues of Stamps

Throughout the foregoing chapters I have referred frequently to the various lists and catalogues of stamps which are currently available to the collector. These vary so much in their scope and the amount of detail which they contain, that I have thought it would be helpful to describe fully the main catalogues which a bird stamp collector would want to know about and consult.

Stanley Gibbons' Stamp catalogues
We in Britain are most fortunate to have a firm of publishers which produces excellent illustrated catalogues of the world's stamps at modest prices. Their catalogues are issued at short intervals—some annually. They are accurate, well-designed and easy to use. From a bird stamp collector's point of view, however, there is one rather disappointing feature. Though quite excellent in all other respects, the SG catalogues use misleading descriptive labels for many of the birds which they list. Their "eagles" frequently turn out to be vultures or falcons, and some of their "falcons" are indisputedly hawks or kites; ibises, herons and spoonbills are apparently completely interchangeable terms; gulls, terns and skuas, tropic birds, boobies, etc. suffer a similar fate, and you will find many others. If a stamp has a scientific and/or English name printed on its surface, that is adopted by the cataloguer, usually without question. This is understandable since one would expect the artist, designer and issuing authority between them to get the name correct. If the stamp has no

names printed on it, the cataloguer should really ensure that the name which he uses is accurate. So, when using SG catalogues, we must remember that whilst their reputation as philatelists is impeccable, they make no claims (and just as well) to be ornithologists.

1. *GIBBONS' Stamps of the World catalogue* Pubd annually.

In one volume, the stamps of the whole world are listed, from the first stamp issued to nearly the end of the previous year. They are arranged by country and under the name of each country or postal authority is given the following information: SG number; year of issue, with event commemorated; denomination; colour/s; price of both mint and used copies of individual stamps, and sets; an illustration of one stamp from the set and notes on the subject of the remaining stamps of the set where these differ. Surface, airmail and postage due stamps are listed together under the country. Exclusions are: local issues or postal labels; details of variations of watermarks and perforations; miniature sheets; fiscal stamps; telegraph stamps.

The Appendix is important because it includes a number of bird stamps with much less detail given about each stamp. Items in the Appendix are "Stamps from countries which either persist in issuing far more stamps than can be justified by postal need or have failed to maintain control over their distribution so that they have not been available to the public in reasonable quantities at face value". Under the name of such countries is a list of dates of issue, name or title of issue, and number of values in the set, and no other information. Since it is thus impossible to find out from the SG catalogue which species are illustrated on those sets listed in the Appendix, it is necessary to use other sources e.g. the American catalogue published by Scott, also W. F. Stanley's *Birds of the World on Stamps*. Countries which have issued bird sets (with the date they were transferred to the Appendix) are: Ajman 1967–72, Bhutan 1968–, Fujeira 1968–, Haiti 1968–, Khor-Fakkan 1965–72, Manama (a dependency of Ajman) 1966–72, Paraguay 1962–, Ras-al Khaima 1968–72, Sharjah 1968–72, Umm-al-Qiwain 1968–, Yemen 1967–.

2. *British Commonwealth Stamp Catalogue* (1978 edn lists stamps 1840–1977). Pubd annually.

Repeats the information in the *Stamps of the World* for each Commonwealth country, but with additional details of printing methods and firms doing the printing; the exact date of issue; perforations; watermark block; designers, miniature sheets, etc. Even greater detail, with illustrations of slight variations is given for Commonwealth stamps issued from 1952–3 onwards in:

3. *Elizabethan Specialised Catalogue of Modern British Commonwealth Stamps* (1978 edn with over 20,200 stamps). Pubd annually.

Adds details of plate varieties, booklets, printings, plate numbers, sheet sizes, imprints, quantities, withdrawal and invalidation dates, paper, etc. This extra information is also given for the section on Great Britain. Under each heading is a short but useful note stating the geographical situation of the country, island or state, its political status, history and currency.

4. *Europe Stamp Catalogue* 3 vols (A–F; G–P; Q–Z)

Information given under name of country includes the exact date of issue and event, designer, watermark, perforations, SG number, denomination (subject of stamp), price of mint and used copies. Under the heading is a note conveying information about that country's geographical position, history and currency.

5. *Overseas Stamp Catalogue* 4 vols (A–C; D–J; K–O; P–Z).

Under the country's name is a note of its history, geographical position and political status. This catalogue includes the usual details, but note also that under the modern name of newly independent colonies, earlier colonial day issues of stamps are included, and where states have combined with others and then separated again, their earlier stamps are also collected under the modern name of the country.

Some collectors will want to supplement these lists by looking at the catalogue of the American philatelic firm, Scott Publishing Co:

Standard Postage Stamp Catalogue 3 vols. Vol. 1. U.S. and affiliated territories, United Nations, British Commonwealth of Nations. Vols. II and III Africa, Asia, Europe, Latin America and Affiliated territories.

The catalogue only lists adhesive postage stamps of the various countries, except for the U.S.A. where additional listings cover revenue stamps and postal stationery. It gives the Scott catalogue number of each individual stamp; denomination; colour; two prices, one used, one unused; variations; year of issue; perforation; watermark; printing method; designer; notes of any special paper. Additional U.S. stamps which are included are: Hunting permit stamps (bearing some very attractive pictures of ducks); Air post stamped envelopes and Official stamp envelopes—including some stylised eagles. Scott lists Air stamps separately (and W. F. Stanley, see below, follows this practice).

Scott uses different forms of names of countries e.g. Jugoslavia; the Netherlands New Guinea appears under West New Guinea (now West Irian). Care must also be taken over the American names for birds.

There have been three unofficial lists of birds on stamps, collated by authors interested in thematic collecting. The first, by W. F. Stanley is an American publication and currently available, whilst the second was compiled by two authors and is now out of print.

1. Willard F. STANLEY *and others Birds of the World on Stamps* 1974 (Handbook No. 82 of American Topical Association, 3306 North 50th Street, Milwaukee, Wis. 53216 $6. When obtained from British stamp shops—£3).

This lists the bird stamps in two ways. First by a scientific classification of bird names (following J. L. Peters *Checklist of the Birds of the World*); Second, A–Z by country. The stamps listed include local issues (Carn Iar; China-Ichang; China-Wuhu; Isle of Canna; Isle of Man; Jethou Is; Kaulbach Is; Lundy; Nagaland; St Kilda; Sanda Is.; and

Stroma Island); the hunting tax stamps of the U.S.A.; the non-Scott items barred for political reasons (North Korea; North Viet-Nam; Cuba; Rhodesia); items from Gibbons Appendix. Items which the authors have been unable to identify are listed in the scientific name list at the end of each Order or Family of birds e.g. "unidentified Psittaciformes". Each unidentified bird stamp is also listed in the country sequence. Stylised birds are not listed in full.

A very useful additional feature in this catalogue of bird stamps is the note alongside each stamp in the classified sequence stating whether the stamp is printed in colour or monochrome. It also indicates whether or not the bird depicted forms the main subject of the stamp (irrespective of the monarch's head, name of country and denomination). These details would enable a collector to select only coloured bird stamps, or to choose only those items where the bird was the main feature of the design, if that is his policy.

This is a very good, full listing of birds on stamps. The American Topical Association members have been publishing material about birds on stamps in their journal *Bio-Philately* for over 20 years and a previous catalogue, also called *Birds of the World on Stamps* was published in 1954. Each issue of the journal gives notes about the birds and animals on new zoological issues and corrects mistakes in naming on the stamps and in catalogues. Many contributors pooled their knowledge and have worked on the identification problems, their aim being to "compile as complete and accurate a list as possible of the wild birds that have been depicted on postage stamps of the world issued through 1972". Some indication of the care taken to establish identities of birds by these enthusiasts is clearly evident in their reference to the 3k Young Thrush stamp of Czechoslovakia 1972. This, they report, cannot be identified since the "Artist is dead. No information on intent is available".

One slight quarrel which a British user would have with this listing, is that the Americans render all sterling currency as "p", whether the old "d" pence or the new decimal "p" pence is meant.

There are just a few identifications in Stanley about which

I have some reservations. However, there are very many identifications in the following book by Strom, which do not agree with the diagnoses in Stanley, and, though I am no expert at bird identification, when comparing the stamp with good pictures in books, it is usually Stanley's identification which stands up to the test. Stanley's nomenclature follows American practice and does not always coincide with British usage e.g. our Great White Heron or Egret *Egretta alba* appears in Stanley under the preferred American name *Casmerodius albus*. The collector in Britain, whilst using the Stanley list must either decide to accept the list as a whole and adopt his nomenclature, or check the scientific and English names against British usage and alter where necessary.

H. STROM & L. H. LEWY *Animals on Stamps.* 1968. Philart Pubns Ltd.

This book, now out of date and out of print, lists animals, snakes, birds, butterflies and insects, which have appeared on postage stamps up to the end of 1967. Strom & Lewy first arrange the species under the name of the country, including illustrations of many sets of stamps, and then list them again, by scientific names.

Strom does not include locals (except Lundy), tax stamps and other etceteras listed in Stanley, but he does include domestic birds. He does not list those stamps with minute portraits of birds flying in the distance, but has concentrated on stamps on which the bird forms a focal point in the design.

He uses nomenclature with which British collectors will be more familiar, but during the last decade the scientists have rearranged and altered so much of the scientific naming of birds as to make his out-dated. Added to this, as stated previously, his diagnosis is open to question in far too many cases to allow any feeling of confidence in accepting his decisions.

LANT, Hugh *Bird Stamps of the World Checklist.* 2nd ed. 1975. (Obtainable from the author, 40 Westbourne Ave., Hull HU5 3HR).

A list of stamps arranged A–Z by name of country. Under the heading is a list of years in which that country issued bird stamps, and following each date is the SG number of the stamp. No further information is given so that it is not possible to discover which bird was illustrated. Gibbons' Appendix items, domestic fowl and poultry are included, but symbolic birds are excluded, also, the author appears to have overlooked a number of genuine wild bird stamps The list goes up to the end of 1974, with a few 1975 items in an appendix.

Stanley Gibbons publish a useful booklet entitled *Complete Index to Foreign Countries and Places*, by James Negus. Available free on request.

Magazines

STAMP MONTHLY Stanley Gibbons' magazine, issued monthly, 40p, in which Gibbons keep their catalogues up to date by listing new issues. News and background information on new issues, articles on design, etc. etc.

BIO-PHILATELY American Topical Association. Subscription in America is $4 per annum and $1 entrance fee for first year. Gives news of new bird stamps, their background and design, and the diagnosis of the species depicted. Compiled by a team of experts.

STAMP COLLECTING WEEKLY 18p from Stamp Collecting Ltd., 42 Maiden Lane, Strand.

STAMP MAGAZINE Monthly 35p Link House Pubrs., Link House, Dingwall Ave., Croydon.

Societies

ROYAL PHILATELIC SOCIETY 41 Devonshire Place, London W.1. Publishes *The London Philatelist* and has a library of 10,000 volumes and 100 periodicals for use by members wishing to do research.

NATIONAL PHILATELIC SOCIETY 1 Whitehall Place, London S.W.1. Publishes *The Stamp Lover*, quarterly.

BRITISH PHILATELIC ASSOCIATION, 1 Whitehall Place, London S.W.1. Publishes *Philately* bi-monthly.

Other magazines and societies exist to cater for the needs of residents in Scotland and Ireland and smaller areas. Their names and addresses can be found at your local public library.

10

Documentation and Research

In earlier chapters, the need to compile your own lists of bird stamps has been mentioned. These are:
1. An alphabetical list of postal authorities, with a list of bird stamps which each country has issued in chronological order under the appropriate heading.
2. A list of the scientific bird names, in exactly the same order as the classification scheme used in the reference book you have chosen as the authority for your stamp collection. Under each species name will be the countries which have issued a stamp depicting that species, with date of issue (and, perhaps, the denomination).

Beyond this basic documentation, there is a great deal of worthwhile information which can be discovered and recorded about each stamp. A thematic collector needs to have space to record information (a) about each stamp and (b) about the bird illustrated on that stamp. Here are some suggestions regarding the points of detail which you may like to establish for the notes you keep about your stamps. Collectively, the notes would lead to the ideal record of a bird stamp collection, however, you may prefer to select only what interests you most and what you think you can handle in the time you have available to spend on your collection.

(a) Details about the stamps
Each stamp will have its own history and relevant information. The country of origin, Gibbons' stamp catalogue number (or other specialist stamp catalogue number), the face value printed on the stamp, the designer, printer and method of printing. Such small details as colour, colour changes,

currency changes, watermarks, perforations, should also be noted, along with the postal history i.e. date of issue, number issued, and date of withdrawal of the stamp and when it was barred from postal usage. Perforation gauges, colour shades (an extremely difficult subject involving tints, depth of ink, etc.), retouches, re-engraving, all create varieties, but these are matters for the experts. The method of printing is always worth a close study, since the results of the many methods used over the last century vary enormously in quality of reproduction—crisp and clear engraving, the softness of lithography, and the tonal qualities of photogravure—all demonstrate clearly the method used, and form an interesting study. Gibbons and Scott both note whether the paper is laid, wove, chalky, etc. but not grades of thickness and colour, so there is scope for investigation there. Phosphor bands (used for postal sorting operations) should also be noted.

How a stamp was issued is also important—whether it was in miniature or full-size sheets, se-tenant, tête-bêche, coil, gum, imperforated, etc.

Different alphabets and numerals, should they prove difficult to understand, may be found at the back of good dictionaries, and Whitaker's Almanack provides a valuable currency guide for each country. There are quite a few stamp books which have definitions of philatelic terms, and which often quote examples and use illustrations of the stamps to elucidate terminology.

The stamp magazines frequently publish articles on how sets were designed and produced, as well as notes on artists and designers and details of varieties and changes. These could be either extracted and placed in your own notes, or if the magazines are kept intact, then a reference made in your notes to the article concerned with a set of stamps.

(b) Details about the birds
You should take all details of the names of the bird from the stamp and the catalogues—noting any mis-spellings, differences in scientific names, and check with the authoritative ornithological work you are using as the basic reference

book for your collection. Account for the differences (e.g. the illustration on the stamp is based on an illustration in an eighteenth century book and the scientific name was copied from the book. The scientific name has been altered since the book was published.) Vernacular names, in all languages, should also be noted and you will build quite a list of these for some of the species. Having established the modern, or currently-used name of the species, add notes as to who is the author of that name, where and when the bird was first described and named. If you have had any difficulty in deciding which species is illustrated, it is as well to record how you finally reached your decision, and which book illustrations you used to reach that decision. The geographical distribution of the species will be of especial interest, because you might well have stamps illustrating one species from all quarters of the globe, or just from one country, perhaps reflecting the bird's range. A life history of the bird would indicate in which part of its range it nests and winters.

Finally, is there any particular reason why that country has chosen to depict that species of bird? Is it nearly extinct in that part of the world, or is it only to be found in a zoo in that country, or has it been adopted as the "national emblem" bird?

Research

Some bird stamps need a great deal of work doing on them to unravel their postal history of varieties, overprints, slight changes in design and colour, etc. Examples of stamps needing careful analysis are some of the early Japanese and Chinese stamps, Guatemala and its Quetzals 1879–1953, New Caledonia and its Kagus, New Guinea's Birds of Paradise, and Uruguay's 32 or so Cayenne Lapwings between 1923 and 1927. Your knowledge of your own collection will indicate other areas in need of greater attention.

An appropriate area for research would be Pigeon Posts. I recently came across a fascinating account of the early New Zealand pigeon-post in a biography of W. B. Tegetmeier (by E. W. Richardson, pubd Witherby 1916), which would make a fine start to an absorbing piece of research into the activi-

ties of these "feathered postmen" as they were called.
Pigeons were used on a surprisingly wide scale to carry letters
and this is most probably why so many stamps of modern
times still depict a pigeon with a letter in its beak. Do these
stamps actually refer back to the days when pigeon posts
were used by that country?

Small special collections, subsidiary to the main collection
and used for intensive study purposes, not only give their
owners additional pleasure, but other people as well. Many
clubs hold exhibitions for which their members make up a
small collection of stamps illustrating a theme. Some of the
stamps in your main collection can be re-mounted for a
special occasion. Alternatively, a small special collection
with a different theme from that of your main collection, can
be built up as a sideline or with an exhibition in mind. The
following themes are offered as suggestions for inexpensive
and easily acquired mini-collections.

Nature Conservation is a topical subject, not just in
Britain, but all over the world, if stamps are anything to go
by. Nature Conservation Year, in 1970, encouraged many
nations to issue a commemorative stamp, or short set, with
pictures of plants, animals and birds in need of protection.
Concern about the protection of nature was shown in other
years, however, e.g. Roumania 1973, Niger Rep. 1959–62,
and Ryu Kyu had a Bird Week in 1966. The allied subject of
pollution was given prominence by the U.S.A. in 1970 with a
"Prevention of Pollution" series, and Monaco's picture of a
polluted seabird in 1971 brought home the danger of oil
slicks on our oceans in a very graphic manner.

National Parks are also featured, where birds in danger of
extinction are carefully reared and protected. The Everglade
National Park harbours the American Great White Heron
(U.S.A. stamp of 1947); Rwanda's Kagera Park protects
three species, all shown on the 40fr stamp of 1965; the Jersey
Wildlife Preservation Trust, founded by Gerald Durrell in
1963, was featured on three stamps illustrating birds
threatened by extinction which are being carefully nurtured
in Jersey (stamps 1971–2); and there are many more inhabi-

Nature Conservation stamps.

tants of nature reserves which have been illustrated to draw attention both to the national parks and the endangered species. "Rare Birds" sets are another way of emphasising the importance of protecting birds' environment e.g. the Seychelles issued a set of 6 stamps showing their rarest species of which only a few pairs remain alive due to encroachment on their habitat.

Species which are known to have died out, appear with "(Ext)" following their names on the stamp. They are a reminder of what could happen if we are not sufficiently concerned to offer protection to endangered species. Cuba issued a set of extinct bird stamps in 1974. Occasionally one extinct bird appears in a set of otherwise live species (see the Philip Island Parrot 25c, 1970 of Norfolk Island) when the illustrations are taken from bird books published some years ago. Anyone wishing to discover which birds are extinct or nearly extinct in order to check their stamps for such species, should consult J. C. Greenway's *Extinct and Vanishing Birds of the World* (New York 1958, a special publication (appropriately No. 13!) of the American Committee for International Wild-life Protection).

In a sense, **zoo sets** form part of a nature conservation collection, because the emphasis nowadays is on breeding rare species in captivity with a view to preserving the species and, if possible, returning some to the wild. Checking through Gibbons' *Stamps of the World* catalogue, it is possible to find quite a number of birds which have appeared in sets of stamps illustrating the inmates of different zoos. Short notes on the zoos, their locality and history, would provide additional interest.

National Emblem Birds. At a conference held in Tokyo in 1960, the following motion was adopted and passed: "Because of its success in bringing the intrinsic value of birds to the attention of the general public, it is urged that each country formally designates a species as its national bird. It is hoped that a list of such birds will be compiled for the next World Conference of the International Council for Bird Preservation." Four years later, eighteen countries had nominated their national emblem birds, but not all of these species have yet appeared on stamps. Those which have appeared are Australia's Kookaburra, America's Bald Eagle, Argentine Republic's Hornero or Rufous Ovenbird, Venezuela's Troupial, Malta's Blue Rock Thrush, Jamaica's Doctor Bird, Ceylon's Jungle-fowl, Mexico's Caracara, South Africa's Blue Crane, Japan's Green Pheasant, Belgium's Kestrel, Uganda's Crowned Cranes, Luxembourg's Goldcrest, Iceland's Gyrfalcon, Sweden's Blackbird and Britain's Robin. The Quetzal is the heraldic symbol or emblem of Guatemala whose coinage is also named after this bird. The Quetzal has appeared on a number of Guatemala's stamps since 1879. Other species to look out for, on future issues, are the Skylark of Denmark, Bellbird of Paraguay, Swallow of Austria, Spoonbill of the Netherlands, White Stork of Germany, Oystercatcher of Northern Ireland, the Nene of Hawaii and the Peacock of India.

National Emblem Birds. Uganda's Crowned Crane 1965; Iceland's Gyrfalcon 1959/60; Argentine's Hornero or Rufous Ovenbird 1966; Australia's Kookaburra 1956; Malta's Blue Rock Thrush 1971.

Naturalists on Stamps. There are very few naturalists whose portraits have appeared on stamps, a regrettable fact when one thinks of the contribution to science which many of them have made. More often, a commemorative issue to honour a naturalist has shown the birds which he drew for publication in books, as we discovered in the chapter on artists and designers.

Albert Engström, Swedish naturalist, with his pet Eagle Owl, Sweden 1969. F. H. A. Baron von Humboldt, a German naturalist who worked in South America from 1799 to 1804, shown with an Andean Condor, Cuba 1969.

One of the greatest bird artists and a very good ornithologist too, was the American, John James Audubon. His portrait was reproduced on a stamp from the U.S.A. in 1940 (S.G.871). In 1969 Sweden honoured Albert Laurentius Johannes Engström (1869–1940) with two stamps (35ö and 50ö) showing him with his Eagle Owl. *Bubo bubo* looks a rather sentimental old bird, but there is no doubt that Engström and Bubo were fond of each other and close companions for a number of years. The Swedish authorities reproduced a self-portrait by this author and painter.

The portrait of a third ornithologist, Count Tomasso A. Salvadori (1835–1923) was reproduced alongside an Australian Cassowary *Casuarius c.* on the Papua, New Guinea 15c value of 1970. The Count had issued a book about the birds of Papua in 1880, and the Papuans honoured him thus when they were hosts to the 42nd Congress of the Australian–New Zealand Association for the Advancement of Science at Port Moresby on 19th August 1970.

It would be nice to know more about these naturalists, and why they were chosen among so many to have their portraits reproduced for a commemorative issue.

* * *

There is so much more to bird stamp collecting than just acquiring the stamps and sticking them in an album. We really know so little about the stamps and the birds they illustrate, that there is scope for a great deal of pleasurable work to be done on them.

Index